Lost Diners and Roadside Restaurants of New England and New York

One cup coming up.

Photo, circa 1920. Interior of dining car, Biddeford, Maine. Courtesy of Maine Historic Preservation Commission, Augusta, Maine.

Over 100 Of The Northeast's
Old-Time Best

Lost Diners and Roadside Restaurants of New England and New York

by Will Anderson

Anderson & Sons' Publishing Co.
34 Park Street
Bath, Maine 04530
(207) 442-7459

A Maine Owned and Operated Company Since 1987

Other Books By The Author

Beers, Breweries & Breweriana (1969)
The Beer Book (1973)
The Beer Poster Book (1977)
Beer, New England (1988)
New England Roadside Delights (1989)
Mid-Atlantic Roadside Delights (1991)
Was Baseball Really Invented In Maine? (1992)
Good Old Maine (1993)
More Good Old Maine (1995)
The Great State Of Maine Beer Book (1996)
Where Have You Gone, Starlight Cafe? (1998)
You Auto See Maine (1999)

Library of Congress Catalogue Card Number 00-092848

Will Anderson 1940 -
1. Popular Culture 2. Diners 3. New England/New York

ISBN 1-893804-01-1

Studio Photography by A. & J. DuBois Commercial Photography, Lewiston, Maine
Typeset and printed by Spectrum Printing and Graphics, Auburn, Maine
Cover lamination by New England Finishing, Holyoke, Massachusetts
Bound by Optimum Bindery Services of New England, Nashua, New Hampshire
Text stock: 100lb. Somerset Gloss Recycled, Sappi North America, Skowhegan, Maine

Cover Design by Jana Kibbe, Spectrum Printing & Graphics
Cover graphic: circa 1940 postcard view,
Champlain Park Cabins & Restaurant,
Shelburne, Vermont

Table of Contents

ACKNOWLEDGEMENTS

Many, many people were good enough to help with the
researching of LOST DINERS AND ROADSIDE RESTAURANTS.
I'd like to especially thank:

Clarence Anspake, Bellmore, N.Y.   Fred Arone, Dobbs Ferry, N.Y.   Mike Barber, Westerly Public Library, Westerly, R.I.
Barbara Barker, Hanover, Mass.   Sharon L. Barnes, Geneva Historical Society, Geneva, N.Y
Kathie Barrie, Portland Public Library, Portland, Me.   Margaret Buckridge Bock, Westbrook, Conn.
Allison Botelho, New Haven Public Library, New Haven, Conn.   Midge Brown, Danbury Public Library, Danbury, Conn.
Mary Lou Buchanan, Brattleboro Historical Society, Brattleboro, Vt.   Donna Burd, Town of Oxford, Oxford, Mass.
Linda Byrne, Wareham Free Library, Wareham, Mass.   Mary Cable, Deposit, N.Y.   Ken Carpenter, Dummerston, Vt.
James M. Carroll, Laconia, N.H.   Al Coleman, Norwood, Ohio   Dean Corner, Patten Free Library, Bath, Me.
Larry Cultrera, Saugus, Mass.   Margaret A. Cunningham, Ellsworth Historical Society, Ellsworth, Me.
Janet Dempsey, Cornwall-on-Hudson, N.Y.   George Dow, Nobleboro, Me.
Betty Eaton, Olean Historical and Preservation Society, Olean, N.Y.   Warren Eddy, Cortland Free Library, Cortland, N.Y.
Helene S. Farrell, Middleburgh, N.Y.   Nancy Finley, The Connecticut Historical Society, Hartford, Conn.
Tom Galvin, Quincy, Mass.   Barbara Gilbert, Town of Rocky Hill, Rocky Hill, Conn.
Frances Gilman, Clinton Historical Society, Clinton, Conn.   Jean Goddard, Franklin County House of History, Malone, N.Y.
Janet Burrows Godwin, Mystic River Historical Society, Mystic, Conn.   Paul K. Graves, Holyoke Public Library, Holyoke, Mass.
Colleen T. Haag, Town of Shelburne, Shelburne, Vt.   H. Leroy Harmon, Blasdell, N.Y.
Elizabeth A. Johnson, Spaulding House Research Library, Pawtucket, R.I.   Kurt Kabelac, Ithaca, N.Y.   Nancy V. Kelly, Rhinebeck, N.Y.
Margaret Ladd, Town of Cazenovia, Cazenovia, N.Y.   Virginia LaGoy, Schenectady County Historical Society, Schenectady, N.Y.
Gregory H. Laing, Haverhill Public Library, Haverhill, Mass.   Karen Lane, Aldrich Library, Barre, Vt.
Karen LaPolice, Town of North Kingstown, North Kingstown, R.I.   Donald LaPlainte, Newburyport, Mass.
Ruth Liberty, Merrimack, N.H.   Charles D. Lord, Bainbridge, N.Y.   Denise MacAloney, Town of Westminster, Westminster, Mass.
Nicholas McCausland, The Rhinebeck Historical Society, Rhinebeck, N.Y.   Frank R. Mooney, Nashua, N.H.
Janet Ottman, Your Home Public Library, Johnson City, N.Y.   Peggy Pearl, Fairbanks Museum, St. Johnsbury, Vt.
Agnes "Pat" Pfleuger, Silver Creek, N.Y.   Liz Reisz, R.W. Traip Academy, Kittery, Me.
Tyler Resch, The Bennington Museum, Bennington, Vt.
Susan Richardson, The Historical Society of the Town of Greenwich, Cos Cob, Conn.   Richard M. Riegel, Cincinnati, Ohio
Randy Roberts, Thomaston, Me.   Robert H. Russell, Town of Wilton, Wilton, Conn.   Dick Shaw, Bangor, Me.
Christine G. Small, East Machias, Me.   Elizabeth L. Somaini, City Hall, Barre, Vt.   Virginia S. Spiller, Old York Historical Society,
York, Me.   Jim and Carol Starkman, Pittsford, N.Y.   Karen Stitt, East Providence Public Library, East Providence, R.I.
Philip M. Strawn, Town of Wareham, Wareham, Mass.   William H. Teschek, Lane Memorial Library, Hampton, N.H.
Carl Timme, Olean Historical and Preservation Society, Olean, N.Y.   Lucy Tranchilda, Groton, Conn.
Lisa von Kann, St. Johnsbury Athenaeum, St. Johnsbury, Vt.   Daniel Zilka, American Diner Museum, Providence, R.I.

PLUS SPECIAL THANKS TO

**Peter D. Bachelder of Ellsworth, Maine, Tom Hug of Vermilion, Ohio, and Earle Shuttleworth and the Maine Historic
Preservation Commission, Augusta, Maine, for their most generous loan of postcard images, and Morgan Mosher of Spectrum
for all his help in putting this book together.**

To Catherine
   From Bath to Buffalo (and Dunkirk, too),
   it sure wouldn't have been as much fun without you.

Preface

For a number of years now I have found myself intrigued by old-time diners and roadside restaurants and cafes: those everyday haunts that have so enriched our lives, spiritually as well as nutritionally. When and why did they open? Whose hopes and dreams were they? How good was their coffee? Their chocolate cream pie?

This book is the result of that intrigue.

The 100-plus eateries that follow – in alphabetical order state-by-state – were chosen because their photo / postcard view and / or ad struck a responsive chord with me. They were places that I found inviting or attractive in one way or another. Places where you could figure on being served a square meal. Places that weren't too fancy or upscale. But that weren't too "down-scale," either. Where your waitress just might look like Jane Powell or Ginger Rogers. Or Jennifer Aniston. "Come as you are" establishments mostly, but with a few chicken-with-all-the-trimmings Sunday dinner spots tossed in, too.

I had planned on titling the book OLD DINERS AND ROADSIDE RESTAURANTS. But as I got into the book and its research I realized that most of the places I was including weren't places that were "old." They were places that were gone. Gone courtesy of Urban Renewal or road widening or the "need" for another bank or parking lot or convenience store or McDonald's, Burger King, Arby's, Applebee's, Red Lobster, etc. I read recently that there are nearly 30,000 KFC, Taco Bell, and Pizza Hut units worldwide. Scary.

LOST DINERS AND ROADSIDE RESTAURANTS, then, pays tribute to those diners and restaurants that are today just a memory. Fallen comrades, if you will. Plus a relatively few that are yet dishing out westerns and easterns, and clam chowder and beef stew, too. Seek out these – and other – survivors. Venture away from the ever boring/ever bland interstate approaches that clutter – and "uglify" – so much of America and you will likely be rewarded with some real delights. Take a break. Patronize them. It's good for them. And it's good for you.

Will Anderson

Will Anderson
Bath, Maine
March 19, 2001

Note: the number of pages devoted to each of the book's seven states is based upon a rough area/population ratio. That's because the more square miles to a state the more miles of road – and roadside – it's apt to have as well. Similarly with population: the more people the more apt there is to be eateries along those miles of road. As an example: Maine and Massachusetts are represented just about even-steven in LOST DINERS. And that's as it should be. Maine has a lot more miles of road while Massachusetts has far and away the more population.

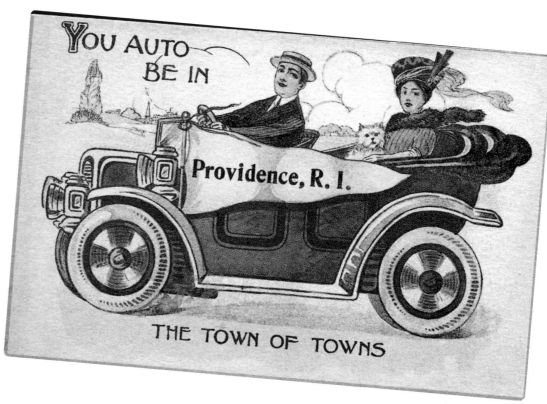

Novelty postcard, circa 1910. When it comes to food, Providence was (and is) a "Town Of Towns." Outside of such towns or cities, however, pickings could be on the slim side during the early days of motoring.

ROADSIDE FARE THROUGH THE YEARS

Eating on the road has seen numerous changes since automobiles started to be here and there and everywhere in the beginning decades of the 20th century. At first, in those pioneering days, if you thought you were going to want a bite while out "motoring" your best bet was to bring that bite with you. Or, should you be passing through a town or city of any magnitude, you could patronize the local cafe, lunch cart, or hotel dining room. By 1910, in fact, many of these citified establishments, especially hotels, began to advertise that they accommodated "automobile parties." That is, they were willing to serve people who arrived by auto – and who might well be covered with dust or caked with mud as a consequence of the road condi-

Ad, THE RED BOOK INTERSTATE AUTOMOBILE GUIDE, 1909. A drive was often called a "run" in those early days of automobiling when piloting a motor car was still very much a sport; even an adventure.

tions of the day – in addition to people who arrived, more traditionally and more elegantly, by rail. "Meals for Automobilists at All Hours," advertised the Norwalk Hotel in Norwalk, Connecticut in 1909, while the Wellswood Hotel, in Hampton Falls, New Hampshire, promised "Special Attention Given to Automobile Parties" that same year.

By the early 1920s a new phenomenon was in the making. Roadside stands began to dot the landscape. Often ramshackle at best and open seasonally – or when someone felt like showing up and opening up – these stands could nevertheless brighten a drive with fresh produce, homemade pies and turnovers, homemade ice cream, soda/pop/tonic, even sandwiches and frankforts. *The Bangor* (Maine) *Daily News* described one such operation in an article in its May 22, 1923 issue. Entitled "Roadside Tea-Rooms Are In Bud," the article told of a farmer outside of Eastport who added to the family income via the sale of various homegrown and/or homemade items. Elaborated the article: "Farmers' families are now giving more attention to refreshment stands erected near their homes and within the month these unique shops have been opened for the auto season (that runs) to late November. Not only is ice cream, fresh from the farms, provided to auto parties, but home cooked foods, fruit, buttermilk, and quick lunches are now on the menu." Concluded the scribe: "With food for the hungry, drink for the thirsty, and rest for the weary, there is now more pleasure for auto parties going into the country."

At about the same time, in the early years of the Roaring Twenties, there appeared overnight cabin complexes. These establishments often included a cafe or lunch room on premises. It made sense: Mr. and Mrs. Motorist could park their Model T, Hudson, or Hupmobile, unload their baggage, then head straight for some hearty lunch or supper fixins. Good examples of such one-stop food/lodging endeavors that adorn the pages of LOST DINERS include the Beverly's (page 44), Birch Knoll (page 45), Cole's (page 50), T Ground (pages 60-61), Wigwam (pages 64-65), the Willows (page 66), Kendall Diner (page 95), the Windmill (page 126), and Babbie's (page 165).

POLLY PRIM

Tea rooms were generally, after the

Elm Hotel,   Meredith, N. H.

Postcard view, circa 1925. By the 1920s "automobilist" business was big time, a fact obviously not wasted on the management of Meredith, New Hampshire's Elm Hotel.

refreshment stand, the first stand-alone eateries to grace the nation's roadways. By "stand-alone" is meant a structure not a part of a cabin court operation and not on a main street in Batavia or Bellows Falls or Woonsocket (although tea rooms could well be there, too). And "grace" may have been just the right word, too…for many a tea room was a converted colonial, Victorian, or "historic" structure. Flower boxes were likely to have been in evidence, as were curtains, linen tablecloths and the like. Often owned and operated by "little old ladies," tea rooms tended to be appreciated by females and not appreciated by males, who often thought both the atmosphere and the portions a little too "dainty." Indeed, there were numerous advertisements for tea rooms in the various auto guidebooks of the 1920s…and many of them did sound "dainty." There was the Blue Gingham Tea Room in Marblehead, Massachusetts, the Polly Prim T House in Redding Ridge, Connecticut, and the Rowley Powley Tea Room in – where else? – Rowley, Massachusetts. The Wayside Tea

"Let's go in and raise hell!"

Cartoon, *Click* magazine, November 1939. Tea rooms were generally the model of sedateness...not the sort of place where anyone would be likely to "raise hell."

Room in Chocorua, New Hampshire, and the Bayview Tea Room in Cornwall-on-Hudson, New York are good examples of tea rooms included in LOST DINERS.

LIGHTS ON FOR SERVICE

Undoubtedly the ultimate in auto-engendered establishments was/is the drive-in restaurant. In all other instances the motorist went to the restaurant. With the drive-in, the restaurant – in the form of carhops – went to the motorist.

The world's first drive-in is generally considered to have been the Pig Stand, opened in September of 1921 on the Dallas-Fort Worth Highway. The idea was the brainchild of a successful Dallas businessman named J.G. Kirby, who is reputed to have declared that "People with cars are so lazy that they don't want to get out of them to eat." J.G. wasn't far off the mark, and drive-ins spread across America from the 1920s through the 1950s. With its short summer season, the northeast never saw the number of drive-ins per capita as did the likes of Florida, Texas, and southern California. But we've had and continue to have our

share. Brunswick, Maine – home to Bowdoin College and Brunswick Naval Air Station: both supplying a solid customer base – is a drive-in hub to this day. It is home to two operating drive-ins, Fat Boy Drive-In (opened in 1955) and Stick To Your Ribs Bar-B-Que & Drive-In (nee Ernie's; in business since 1949). Old-time drive-ins represented in LOST DINERS are Danny's in Schenectady (page 141) and the Knotty Pine in Bennington (page 173).

HO-JO'S, FRIENDLY'S, AND DUNKIN' DONUTS, TOO

The latest in the evolution of on-the-road fare is, of course, the limited menu / fast food movement. Here the northeast, for better or probably worse, has contributed mightily. That once king-of-the-hill, Howard Johnson's (with fried clams and grilled frankforts and 28 flavors of ice cream from which to choose), first saw the light of day in the Wollaston section of Quincy, Massachusetts in 1925. Friendly's was begun by brothers Curt and Pres Black in Wilbraham, Massachusetts in 1935. Then there's Quincy again: it was home to the nation's very first Dunkin' Donuts in 1950. Even that giant of giants in the

Photos, October 2000. Both located on the Bath Road in Brunswick, Maine, Fat Boy and Stick To Your Ribs are a pair of drive-in classics. Fat Boy's name comes from the fact that original proprietor John Bollinger had seen the name out west, liked it, named his own place that when he opened in 1955. Stick To Your Ribs was born as Ernie's in 1949; remained Ernie's until purchased by new proprietor John Gerken in February 2000. Between them Fat Boy and STYR have 98 years under their belt. That's a lot of cheeseburgers.

franchise fast-food world – McDonald's – had its origins in the northeast. Sort of. Its founding fathers, brothers Richard and Maurice "Mac" McDonald, were natives of New Hampshire.

THERE'S NOTHING FINER THAN EATING IN A DINER

So what have we forgotten in this brief excursion down the road of roadside eating? The answer: the "sexiest" category of them all...the diner. Strangely though, while the diner is generally beloved as the most "roadside" of all eateries, it really isn't. Its origins well predate the coming of the automobile. And its location was more often than not a downtown setting, wedged into the fabric of Main Street or a mill complex. Still, the diner has such charm, such "zing," that it has captured the heart of a never-ending parade of folks who enjoy the diner's intimate atmosphere and its tradition of an honest meal for an honest price. It's well worth the time, therefore, to pay special tribute to the diner and the fact that it was born deep in the heart of not Texas, not southern California, not Detroit. No, the diner was born deep in the heart of New England.

Circa 1950 diner
matchbook
advertising art

THE DINER: IT'S AN OLD NEW ENGLAND INVENTION

Before there was the dining car/diner there was the lunch wagon or, as it was often called, the night lunch or night owl. Its beginnings go back – way back – to 1872 when one Walter Scott of Providence, Rhode Island converted a horse-drawn freight wagon into a horse-drawn lunch wagon and set out to sell boiled eggs, homemade sandwiches, and pies and hot coffee to Providence's latenighters. It was Yankee ingenuity at its tastiest. And it worked: "Scotty" did a brisk business, causing other entrepreneurs to stake out their own routes and locations. Some of these "others" made improvements as well. This was especially true in nearby Worcester, Massachusetts. A Worcesterite by the name of Sam Jones created a wagon that was large enough for patrons to come inside to eat. Next came another Worcesterite, Charles Palmer, who envisioned success for the lunch

A Trio We've Enjoyed

Although New England has lost far too many of her diners, there are yet over 200 in operation. Here's a southern New England trio Catherine and I have enjoyed: Betsy's Diner (Falmouth, Mass.); Central Diner (Millbury, Mass.); and the Winsted Diner (Winsted, Conn.). That's Bob Radocchio, the Winsted's proud proprieter for 28 years, in front of his "baby." All photos, spring 2000.

wagon far beyond the cozy confines of New England. He set up a lunch wagon *manufacturing* company. That was in 1891. Yet another Worcester resident, Thomas H. Buckley, went a step farther by not only producing, but *mass* producing, the wagons. By the late 1890s, thanks in large part to Buckley's efforts, there were lunch wagons plying the streets in towns and cities across most of America. And as prestigious a newspaper as *The Chicago Tribune* went so far as to feature the lunch wagon – which they dubbed the "sandwich car" – in a long article in their Sunday edition of July 5, 1896. All these many, many decades later what *The Tribune* had to say still makes for some interesting reading.

"Like many other curious and useful institutions the 'sandwich car' first made its appearance in Chicago in 'World's Fair Year.' (editorial note: the Columbian Exposition / World's Fair took place in 1892-1893). Briefly described, it is a kitchen and restaurant on wheels, much in the form of an elongated carette (editorial note: THE OXFORD ENGLISH DICTIONARY defines "carette" as an obsolete form of the word "cart."), but having a larger window space on all four sides. It is drawn by a single horse to the spot where it stands for the night, usually to some saloon corner near what is termed a 'sporting neighborhood,' and there it may be found winter and summer, fair weather or stormy, until about 5 o'clock in the morning. In fact, the sandwich man pays a tax of $5 monthly to the saloonist for this privilege, although there is no city tax or license fee on the business and no other formality in starting it save a gracious 'permission' from the

Ad from the 1895 edition of THE GARNET, the yearbook of Union College, Schenectady. While today "lunch" generally refers to a mid-day meal it formerly meant a light meal at any hour.

Captain of the police precinct. On this basis may now be counted about a score of sandwich cars located at the intersections of State, Madison, Clark, and Harrison streets and Archer, Milwaukee, Cottage Grove, and Blue Island avenues.

The cars are painted all over white, the panels below the glazed portion usually being inscribed 'Lunch Car' and in some cases with the bill of fare that is offered to the 'children of the night.' Within the car, ordinarily, is a three-burner gasoline range, a steaming closet, recesses for dish washing, and kitchen appliances and an arrangement of shelves for displaying the most tempting edibles to the gaze of the passer-by. The whole is lighted with kerosene lamps, and sometimes a gasoline torch, giving to the

It's not Chicago. It's Potsdam, New York. But it affords a splendid view of a circa 1900 lunch wagon. To attract attention, many such wagons were done up in fancy – even florid – designs, often complete with stained glass windows. A fine example, indeed, was Potsdam's Eat-a-Bite Wheel Cafe, shown here with proprietor Benjamin Miles at the dawn of the 20th century. Photo courtesy of Potsdam Public Museum, Potsdam.

stationary vehicle a festive, circus-like aspect and inevitably winning the attention of the hungry and the curious who may chance along the sidewalk. Everything within is as bright and clean as soapsuds can make it, and the caterer or his wife is neatly garbed and aproned in restaurant style. The vendor is at once cook, waiter, and cashier.

The pièce de résistance is a chicken sandwich, which consists of a quarter section of a small spring chicken, cold, placed between two slices of bread, with the accompaniment of a pickle, a green onion, or a dash of catsup. This costs 10 or 15 cents. Pork chops, ham, pig's feet (fresh or pickled), fried fish, codfish cakes, and eggs are also put in sandwich form, mostly at five cents each. A distinguished favorite, only five cents, is Hamburger steak sandwich, the meat for which is kept ready in small patties and 'cooked while you wait' on the gasoline

THE GREAT PORTLAND NIGHT LUNCH "WAR"

Where there's money to be made there's generally competition to be found. A fine example of this, with respect to the night lunch "industry," took place in Portland, Maine at and around the turn-of-the-20th-century. In 1892 a man named Patrick H. McNamara opened a night lunch on Federal Street in the downtown district of "the Metropolis of Maine." For five years he appears to have had the trade to himself. In 1897, however, along came a woman named Alice F. Merrill, who opened up a competitive wagon. From then on both parties did their darndest to try to outdo the other. By 1902, the year of the two ads pictured here, the pair had worked their way up to seven locations between them...four for Alice and three for Mac.

In 1906 Mac dropped out of the race, becoming a druggist instead. Alice, though, kept on. She ran night lunches all the way through to 1919. Some say her spirit – if not her nice coffee and hot baked beans – still lingers when the moon is full in the Port City.

Both ads are from a recipe booklet published by the Woman's Relief State Corps, Portland, 1902.

Circa 1950 diner matchbook advertising art

range. Fried oysters, breaded, are also a popular sandwich ingredient.

The sandwich man takes in from $5 to $7 a night, perhaps $12 on Saturday or other special nights – this 'special' implying when many people are out late – and makes an average profit of 25 percent on his outlay, say $12 a week, besides much of the food required for himself and family. Many of them keep no horse, but hire one at 50 cents a day to haul the sandwich car to and from its nightly stand. It is a business principle of them to sell out everything, if necessary even at a startling reduction, before going home in the morning, so that supplies for the next night may all be fresh cooked."

Over 100 years later many of *The Tribune's* words still ring remarkably true. An 1896 "sandwich car." A year 2001 dining car. They're not so different in a lot of respects. What, after all, is 105 years?

CONNECTICUT

Area: 5009 sq. miles. Population: 3,405,565

Scale: 1 inch = approximately 11 miles

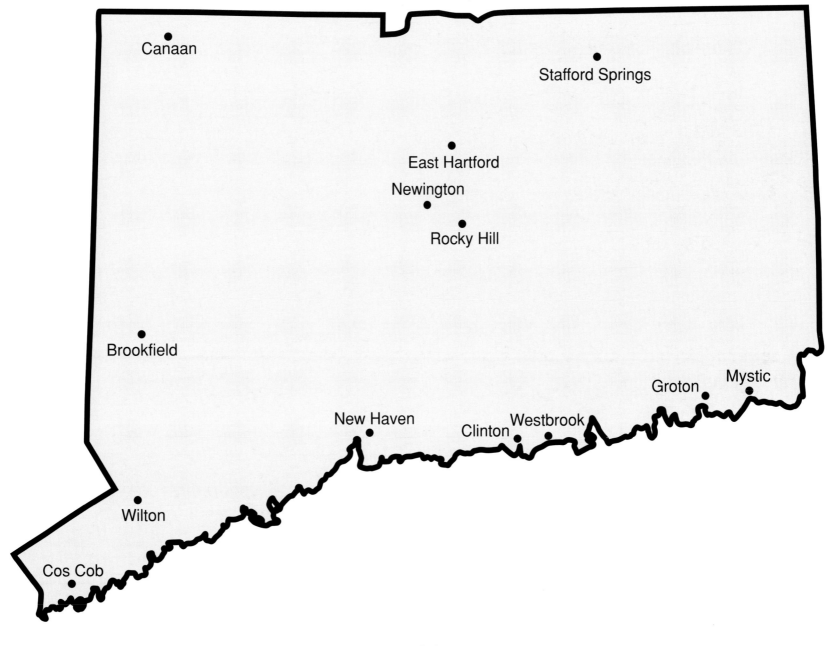

Photo, 1926. Courtesy of Library of Congress, Washington, D.C.

CANAAN LUNCH
CANAAN

Canaan had it all in this marvelous 1926 photograph. You could buy a Reo (named after Ransom E. Olds, the man who also created the Oldsmobile). You could catch a double feature at the Colonial. Or you could dine at the Canaan Lunch.

Opened on December 29, 1924, the Canaan Lunch operated until just after the end of World War II. There are those around town who still recall it. Local historian Fred J. Hall rounded up a bunch of those who do. Here's what he reports: "It was a popular restaurant serving the ordinary people, open 24 hours a day, seven days a week. It was very popular with truck drivers during the night traveling Route 7."

Small, with a counter and stools and a few oil-cloth bedecked tables, "It was always neat and clean." Beef stew was a specialty. Another specialty was home-made apple pie. Then there were hamburgers, too, with beef from a butcher shop located not 100 feet down the street.

Circa 1946, alas, the Canaan Lunch's land was deemed more valuable not having the Canaan Lunch on it. The structure pictured here was torn down, with a garage built in its place.

THE CLAM BOX
COS COB

The Clam Box opened on Memorial Day 1939, the dream of George and Anna Gross, who invested $200.00 to construct a just-the-basics seafood stand on the Boston Post Road (U.S. Route 1). Designed to be summer only, the stand did such a brisk business the couple found themselves almost immediately enlarging it and going year 'round. Branch operations in Westport (1940-1981) and Wethersfield (1940-1980) were not far behind.

After eight years in their original location, George and Anna moved their flagship restaurant. Still on the Post Road and still in Cos Cob, the couple's new set-up was sizable, but not sizable enough. George and Anna made an addition here, and an addition there and, by the time the postcard shown here was printed, the Clam Box was billed as "New England's Largest Seafood Restaurant." Lobster, crabs, oysters, and "The Belly Burster" (a huge plate of mixed sea food and French fries) were all top sellers.

The Clam Box's future began to unravel in the 1980s. An I-95 bridge over the Mianus River collapsed in June 1983, causing monumental traffic tie-ups and the loss of considerable business. Rising real estate values, though, were the major culprit. In the end – which was 1985 – George and Anna's son Arthur decided to sell the restaurant and the 1.8 acres on which it sat for a cool $3.5 million or so. The eatery the Grosses had built into an institution was demolished and a 39-unit condominium constructed in its place. Its official name: "Greenwich Court." Its unofficial name: "Clam Box Condos."

Sea Food at its Best
The Clam Box

On The Post Road
on U. S. No. 1
Cos Cob   Conn.

Postcard view, circa 1955. The Clam Box was big: big enough to be ballyhooed as "New England's Largest Seafood Restaurant."

FREDA FARMS
NEWINGTON

There's a word for a building that's shaped the same as that which it sells. That word is "programmatic." Freda Farms was very definitely programmatic. They sold ice cream. One glance at its ice cream carton design and you knew that. Begun in 1931 by three partners – Homer Messier, James Donaghy, and Oscar Epstein, all of New Bedford, Massachusetts - who had vivid imaginations and/or loved ice cream, Freda Farms stood out even on that strip of strips, the Berlin Turnpike. "It hit you right in the eye as you came along, that's for sure," chuckled longtime Turnpike aficionado Harry Mandell when I asked him about the stand.

At the start only ice cream and ice cream specialties were sold. Sandwiches, hot dogs, and the like were added, however, within the initial year. At first Freda Farms was just a take out and car service stand, too. Success

Photographs, both October 1939 and both courtesy of the Library of Congress.

changed that. A large July 2, 1932 *Hartford Courant* ad featured a sketch of a newly enlarged operation and beamed "To accommodate the many people desirous of inside service it is our privilege to announce the opening tonight of an addition providing booths to accommodate one hundred people." The addition of a chef to the staff was also announced…"to enable us to offer an increased variety of Toasted Sandwiches."

With World War II making it difficult to obtain sugar (for ice cream) and gas (for patron's autos), Freda Farms closed "for the duration" in 1943. It was reopened, by Benjamin and Ernest White, in 1946, and remained in operation, under various proprietors, until 1966. At some point after that the building, marvelous as it was to the eye, was demolished. On its former site, 2530 Berlin Turnpike, there is now a hodge-podge of structures housing Carefree Gazebos and Small Buildings.

THE FOUNTAIN ROCKY HILL

Unique as it would seem to have been, Freda Farms' structure appears not to have been so unique after all. A *very* similar stand was opened in Rocky Hill a year earlier, in 1930. Known as the Fountain, that structure still stands, minus the decorative touches, as VFW Post 2138. It's worth a drive down Route 99 (old Route 9) to admire it.

Photo, December 1999

Photos, June 1956. Courtesy of the Connecticut Historical Society, Hartford. Gordon's was not lacking with respect to signage.

GORDON'S DINER
NEW HAVEN

It's difficult to go too far wrong with the name "Yale" in New Haven. Such was most likely the thinking of Samuel Sachlos when he opened his Yale Diner in 1939. And Yale the diner remained until Ethel Gordon, a former New York, New Haven & Hartford Railroad restaurant worker, came along in 1954. Then the Yale Diner became Gordon's Diner.

Ethel ran her diner, seemingly successfully, until it was gutted by fire in or around 1957. Its old address, at 98 Forbes Avenue, is now occupied by a series of small fuel storage tanks. Not far up the street, though, is the Forbes Diner, a Fodero (built by the former Fodero Dining Car Company, Bloomfield, New Jersey) that keeps the diner tradition alive and well on Forbes Avenue. It opened in 1958, just after Gordon's closed.

JILL'S DINER
GROTON

"He was out of the service and he wanted to make money and it (the former Gus' Diner) was there and it was for sale." So relates Jill (D'Angelo) Caracausa as to how her brother, New London-native Pasquale "Totsy" D'Angelo, came to start Jill's in 1946. "And he named it after me," she says proudly.

At first Totsy and Jill ran the whole show themselves. Then they hired Cora Dewey. It paid off. "She was some cook," continues Jill. "We had good food. Really good food. We used to make beautiful clam chowder. And fish and chips. Big time portions, too. We had three pieces of fish. We made our own French fries, too." Seventy-eight year old Lil Garcia agrees. "They had the best hamburgers in town," says Lil. "A group of us girls used to go duckpin bowling. And after that we'd go have a cup of coffee and a hamburger (at Jill's). That was our weekly ritual."

Totsy and Jill and Cora ran Jill's, located at 7 Thames Street, until 1958 when they sold to another man named Pasquale, Pasquale Groccia. Groccia kept the Jill's name until 1963, when he changed it to Jay's. It later, in 1966, was purchased by Norm Brochu (who then owned and still owns Norm's Diner, a 1954 Silk City that sits up the hill at 171 Bridge Street). Norm changed the diner's name one last time, to the Circle Diner. "It was on the Route 1 traffic circle," he explains. In 1970 Norm was, unfortunately, in a bad auto accident. Incapacitated for six months, he could not handle the running of both diners. He sold the Circle. After being utilized for a time for storage, the old diner was demolished. On the site now is an office building.

Matchbook cover, circa 1950. Jill Caracausa: "And he named it after me."

LOUIS DINER
STAFFORD SPRINGS

Where the Louis Diner used to be – you can see both the diner and its hanging sign in the left center of the scene shown here – there is now an empty lot. The outline of the diner, however, is still in evidence on the side of the building just to the diner's right. The proprietor of the nearby Ideal Package Store, Candy Hauschulz, proudly pointed it out. Candy also introduced me to the regulars at the down-the-block Arizona Restaurant. They all well-recalled the diner; that it was often called "Marty's;" that it "just disappeared" one day in the late 1950s. Joe Paradiso, 65, recalls Louis best. "I delivered papers there. The *Hartford Courant.* It would've been 1944-1945." Then a good smile comes across Joe's face: "Mrs. Tonidandel was my best tipper. She'd give me 50¢ a week plus there was always a standing invitation to have a doughnut." Why the generosity? Joe smiles again: "I was a good paperboy and she was a nice woman."

Marty (aka "Mario") Tonidandel sold Louis Diner to local entre-prenuer George Bartlett in June 1950. "He (George) was looking for something to get into where he'd be his own boss." recalls George's son Dave. The diner, however, turned out to be "something" George didn't do long. "I think it was too much," reflects Dave. "They (George and his wife Alice) got out of the restaurant business fairly soon." In September 1951, to be exact. After a few others gave it a try, Marty Tonidandel resumed the operation of the diner in 1953 and operated it until circa 1956. By then he was far more interested in his other venture, Marty's Hardware. The diner, which sat adjacent to the hardware store, was put into service as a storage bin. Then, come 1959, it was gone. "Just disappeared," as the gang at the Arizona phrased it.

MAIN ST. STAFFORD SPRINGS, CONN.

Postcard view, circa 1935. Courtesy of Dave Bartlett, Stafford Springs.

CONNECTICUT

Photograph, circa 1945. Courtesy of Dave Bartlett, Stafford Springs.

"It Was The Hamburgs"

"My husband Marty was about 19 when his father, Louis, bought the diner for him. Louis was always interested in diners. He used to stop in at this big diner in the Hartford area and that's where he got the idea of bringing a diner to town. I can recall the day it came by freight (railroad) and then came up Main Street through town. It was a big thing. There weren't many diners then. That would've been in 1926-1927. I know it was before the Depression.

"It (the diner) was very popular. The hamburgers were what everybody wanted. Then there was beef stew and a daily special. But it was the hamburgs they couldn't get enough of."

Interview with 90-year old Anna Tonidandel, Stafford Springs, June 2000.

IT'S GOOD STUFF.

Stafford Springs is one of a handful of Connecticut communities that yet have an in-operation independent bottling works. Located near the Stafford Motor Speedway, Stafford Springs Soda Company produces 15 flavors. *Real* flavors like black cherry, birch beer, strawberry, and peach. Stop by and see the company's display of old soda pop bottles and labels. And buy a case or two of whatever assorted flavors tickle your fancy. It's good stuff.

Postcard view, circa 1932. The "Diner Deluxe" before its Clinton cousin
was added on. Courtesy of Helen and Jim Verry, Westbrook.

MODERN GRILL
WESTBROOK

It didn't take Frank Verry (please also see page 83) long to figure out that good diner fare could pave his road to success. Arriving in America in 1922 when he was 17, the Italian native went to work almost immediately as a short order cook / counterman / jack-of-all-eatery-trades in the Westerly, Rhode Island / Pawcatuck, Connecticut area. Mostly Frank worked for Crist Ferraro, also a native of Italy. Together the two ran the Modern Grill in Pawcatuck from 1929 on. Business was good and, circa 1931, Crist and Frank opened a sister operation, also called the Modern Grill, in Clinton. Again the duo met with success, which led to the need for more space. This they accomplished in a novel way. First, circa 1932, they purchased a brand new, double-long diner and had it delivered to neighboring Westbrook. Then they had their Clinton diner picked up and also moved to Westbrook. They then joined the two. And nicknamed their creation the "Diner Deluxe."

Around 1933 Frank purchased Crist's shares in the Westbrook operation. On his own at last, Frank really shined. "He never came to work without a white shirt and tie," recalls his widow, Helen. "He thought that to be before the public he should look neat and professional. He," continues Helen, "took great pride in his diner and the people

Snapshot, circa 1947. Frank, who passed away in 1982, with several of his employees and his ever-present tie. Courtesy of Helen and Jim Verry, Westbrook.

he served. And the people he hired," she adds. "It was like a family."

Seafood was Frank's specialty. Especially his scallops. Helen again: "I remember the scallop special.

French fries and cole slaw, and scallops falling off the plate."

Frank, who closed the Modern during World War II when he was in the U.S. Army, had long promised

Interior view postcard, circa 1940. The Modern sold Kings (see sign, upper left), a beer brewed in Brooklyn from 1933 to 1940. Its slogan: "Fit For A King."

himself an early retirement. In 1950 he kept that promise. He sold the diner to a man named Everett "Andy" Anderson. Andy, however, soon decided he didn't want to run such a big restaurant. So he slowly but surely converted the larger diner into a motel, with the smaller original unit used for storage. Sounds crazy…but it worked. Drive along the Boston Post Road/U.S. Route 1 on the western outskirts of Westbrook today and you'll see, at number 756, the Modern Grill reincarnated as the Viking Motel.

MODERN GRILL MYSTIC

In addition to Pawcatuck, Clinton, and Westbrook, Crist Ferraro (1888-1977) was involved in at least one other Modern Grill. That was in Mystic. This is how it looked just after the Hurricane of 1938 (that's water, not roadway, in front of the diner) had pounded New England.

Photo, September 1938. Courtesy Jesse B. Stinson Collection, Mystic River Historical Society, Mystic.

THE WAGON WHEEL
BROOKFIELD

The Wagon Wheel, which evolved out of a frozen custard stand, was one of a handful of dine and dance "hot spots" that enlivened U.S. Route 7 north of Danbury in the late 1930s and 1940s. There was the Twin Cedars, the Dutch Mill ("Gala Floor Show and Dancing"), the Village Barn ("Connecticut's Swankiest Inn"), the Wagon Wheel, others.

The Wagon Wheel (later Lavelle's Wagon Wheel) gives me the rare opportunity to interview myself. I lived in western Connecticut from 1970 to 1980. For about half that time, 1971 to 1975, I was privileged to host a weekly 1950s' oldies show. Called the Rockin' and Rollin' Party,* it was broadcast over radio station WINE (now far better known as I-95), located next door to the Wagon Wheel. From time to time I'd invite a guest record collector to join me on the show, to share his/her favorites. Guests came from all over Connecticut, the Hudson River valley, Long Island, even Haverhill, Massachusetts and Newark, New Jersey. After the show we'd inevitably repair to the Wagon Wheel. There we'd enjoy a pizza and a brew or two. But mostly we'd discuss the music we loved and the wonders of the likes of the Moonglows, Cardinals, Little Richard, Mac Curtis, Buddy Holly & the Crickets, (Connecticut's own) Nutmegs, Fi-Tones…and the Heartbeats ("Crazy For You"/"A Thousand Miles Away"), Bill Haley & the Comets ("Rock Around The Clock" / "Shake, Rattle And Roll" / "Dim, Dim The Lights"), Gene and Eunice ("Ko Ko Mo" / "This Is My Story"), Gene Vincent & the Blue Caps ("Be Bop A Lula"/"Lotta Lovin' "), and, best of all, Fats Domino ("Ain't It A Shame"/"Blue Monday" /"Blueberry Hill"/"Poor Me"/lots more).

It was grand!

WAGON WHEEL INN
Danbury-New Milford Road — Route 7, Brookfield, Conn.
Excellent Food — Choice Wines and Liquors — Dancing
H. J. Bussiere, Prop.

Postcard view, circa 1945

CONNECTICUT

It's now over a quarter of a century later. I've long since moved from western Connecticut. The radio station has moved, too. The Heartbeats et al. don't get nearly the airplay they should. The Wagon Wheel, however, is yet at its old familiar stand, although it's no longer named the Wagon Wheel. It's now, looking much the same, Rosalia's Ristorante.

*Later, from 1995 to 1997, revitalized as the Big Daddy Rockin' & Rollin' Party over WXGL, Freeport-Portland, Maine. It was grand all over again!

Fats

The Heartbeats

Gene & Eunice

Gene Vincent

Bill Haley

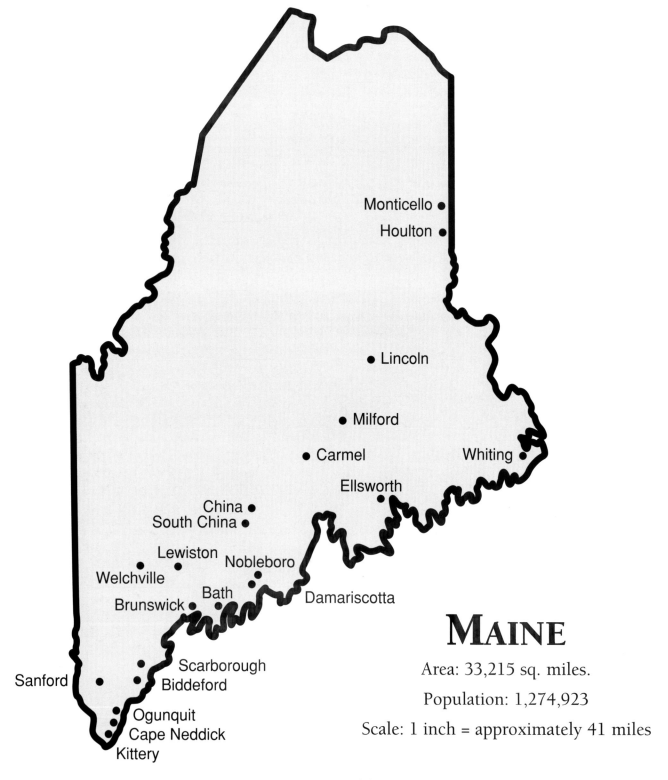

Monticello ●

Houlton ●

● Lincoln

● Milford

● Carmel   Whiting ●

Ellsworth ●

China ●
South China ●

Lewiston ●
Welchville ●   Nobleboro
Bath
Brunswick ●   Damariscotta

Scarborough
Sanford   Biddeford

Ogunquit
Cape Neddick
Kittery

MAINE

Area: 33,215 sq. miles.

Population: 1,274,923

Scale: 1 inch = approximately 41 miles

AL'S DINER
LEWISTON

It's been over 40 years since Louis Dumont helped out at his dad's diner after school, but Louis still clearly recalls the diner's specialty of the day for every day. Monday was ham and spinach; Tuesday was American chop suey; Wednesday was corned beef hash; Thursday was New England boiled dinner; Friday was fried clams; Saturday was baked beans and franks. The latter was "a big, big thing," Louis points out. "And the boiled dinner: that was another biggie."

Albert "Al" Dumont was a cook in the service during World War II. At war's end he came home raring to cook some more. The former Bill White's Diner was up for sale. Albert bought it in 1946, changed its name to "Al's," and was open from 5:00 AM to 8:00 PM every day except Sunday. Situated at 53 Bates Street in front of the Knapp Shoe plant, Al's enjoyed a hefty trade from the many mill workers then in the area. He did well with the numerous trucking companies in the neighborhood, too.

All went well until 1961 when Knapp Shoe, from whom Albert leased the land his diner was on, announced they needed the parcel for a new loading dock. Al's was demolished. Albert, himself, started another venture, Al's Lunch, elsewhere in Lewiston. He then worked as a cook in one eatery or another until his retirement in 1976. He died, aged 75, in 1991.

Photo, circa 1958. That's Albert Dumont in front of his diner in front of Knapp Shoe. Courtesy of Louis Dumont, Lewiston.

ARROW RESTAURANT
NOBLEBORO

The Arrow Restaurant (aka the Arrow Diner) was part of a complex that at one time or another included a sizable inn (the Glendon Inn), a cabin cluster (the Arrow Camps), and 300 acres. It was purchased in 1946 by Emery and Katherine Henny, a young couple of Hungarian descent from New Jersey. Soon thereafter Katherine opened the Arrow on a portion of their property adjacent to U.S. Route 1, the old Atlantic Coast Highway. Emery raised chickens.

The Arrow was not large. An account of the time describes it as "small but perfectly equipped and exquisitely kept." With Katherine's brother Louis Schweitzer doing the cooking, the Arrow advertised "The Best in Home Cooked Food." Emery and Katherine's son George recalls there were chicken, turkey, and roast beef dishes. Plus seafood and Hungarian meals as well. Breakfast, lunch, and dinner were all served.

A bad fire in the inn/guest house in 1960 translated to fewer customers in the restaurant. Plus Emery was in poor health. (He would pass away in 1965). The Arrow served its last meal in 1963. The building that housed it was moved to become part of a home for George. It is today still a private residence.

Postcard view, circa 1950. Courtesy Peter D. Bachelder, Ellsworth

Auto Rest Park, Carmel, Maine   Eleven Miles West of Bangor

From a postcard view, circa 1940. Back when Route 2 was Maine's major east-west artery and Auto Rest Park was *the* place to go.

AUTO REST PARK
CARMEL

In 1921 Charles E. Adams, Bangor's pioneer all day/all night lunchroom man ("When the history of the restaurant business in Bangor is written 'Charlie' Adams deserves a chapter": *The Bangor Daily News*, 6/7/24), branched out and opened Auto Rest Park. At first a jumbled auto camp, filling station, and tourist-amusing bevy of reptiles, the Auto Rest was purchased by Harry and Lizzie Wise in early 1924. Under their direction it blossomed until it was a veritable Route 2 one-stop gas/food/lodging/entertainment mecca. A man who remembers those days well is 84-year old Ward Shaw. A native of Milo, Ward played a mean trumpet in the Perley Reynolds' Orchestra when Perley and his gang were Saturday night regulars at the Auto Rest's

ballroom in the late 1930s. "Everybody went there (to the Auto Rest). They took their families and they'd ride the merry-go-'round and eat ice cream, hot dogs, and hamburgers. And dance," adds Ward proudly. "It was *the* place to go, it was," he sums up.

Hard times eventually came to Ward Shaw's old haunt. Fire, a collapsed roof, changing traffic patterns: all took their toll. Not much remains nowadays. Part of the old "EAT" building is incorporated into the structure, Brent's Auto Center, that occupies much of the Auto Rest's old site. But you'd be hardpressed to find it.

43

Postcard view, circa 1930. Courtesy of Peter D. Bachelder, Ellsworth. This structure still stands, albeit in a new location further downeast, in Edmunds. Sad to say it is minus its front porch. There was a not-very-wide bridge on the structure's route to its new home. It a case of widen the bridge or remove the porch. The porch lost.

THE BEVERLY'S
WHITING

Arthur Beverly started it all by purchasing the site you see here, just over the East Machias line in Whiting, in 1926. Soon thereafter he appears to have built the structure you also see here. He named it The Beverly's and pumped gas and served, with help from daughters Ruth and Marjorie, standard lunchroom fare. In 1935 Bertha Flynn and her husband Ed took over. They changed the name to the Lakeview (the name it would keep ever after). Bertha did all the cooking and serving in the lunchroom. Ed built overnight cabins to increase cash flow. (Notes local historian Christine Small: "The Flynns had four children, all young, and they ate lots of the profits!").

Quite a few other owner/operators tried their hand at the roadside complex. A circa 1950 brochure pictures the lunchroom and a row of tidy cabins, and boasts "Breakfast and Dinners"/"Home Cooking"/"Heated Cabins"/"Hot and Cold Water."

Operations ceased – no one really knows why – in the mid-1960s. Since then the buildings have been slowly sold off and moved away. The former lunchroom now resides in Edmunds where it serves as an office for the summer science field station of Boston's Suffolk University. Two of the overnight cabins also now call Edmunds home. Two were moved to Jonesboro. One yet remains in Whiting. One has disappeared.

BIRCH KNOLL
CAPE NEDDICK (YORK)

In 1920, before Route 1 had become Route 1 (that would happen in 1926), Celia and William Norton rounded up $2,500 and purchased 10½ acres of land fronting on what was then called the State Road and started building. "William built everything himself," states distant nephew Ken Young. "First came a house and then came a string of cabins. He just kept building as he had money."

The restaurant came along circa 1930. Ken, who ate there as a youngster in the mid-1940s, recalls it as small and featuring "just good home cooking. Celia was a hell of a cook: one of those old-fashioned cooks who'd have a handful of this and a handful of that. She never measured...she just knew."

Around the time Ken was partaking of Celia's good cooking, Celia was, ironically, winding down the restaurant. "It just got to be too much for her," reasons Ken.

In the mid-1950s, the Nortons added on to the former restaurant and turned it into a grocery store. According to Rich Young, Celia and William's great-grandson and co-proprietor today, the store ceased being run in the 1970s. The cabins, though, are still very much in operation. As for the former restaurant structure, it presently houses the office for the cabins as well as a pair of apartments. Rich, though, is considering turning the structure into a lobster pound. "Sort of an outdoor lobster bake," he explains. Time will tell.

BIRCH KNOLL CABINS
ROUTE 1, CAPE NEDDICK, MAINE
Running hot and cold water—showers. Cooking privileges or restaurant. One mile to surf bathing, Ogunquit Beach.
MRS. W. C. NORTON, Mgr.

Ad, circa 1940

Photo, circa 1935. Courtesy of the Maine Historic Preservation Commission, Augusta. The gas pumps are gone and so is Tydol, but most everything else pictured here is yet intact (or enlarged, as with the old lunchroom).

THE BON TON — LINCOLN, MAINE

Postcard view, circa 1950. The Bon Ton's facade was modernized to look as it appears here around 1950. Before that, Walter Cameron, a Lincoln native all of his almost 90 years, told me "it had a plain, plain front." Primarily a restaurant and lounge, the Bon Ton served as a hotel, too, with 16-18 rooms upstairs.

THE BON TON
LINCOLN

"Bon Ton" translates roughly, in English, to "fashionable or stylish." When it came to Lincoln's Bon Ton, however, that was and wasn't true. That's because Lincoln's Bon Ton was, as worded so vividly by 77-year old Kenwood Boyington, "a restaurant and a beer joint at the same time." John Swanson, 70, is a little more genteel: he characterizes the Bon Ton as having been "a restaurant and cocktail lounge."

Actually, the Bon Ton opened when there were neither "beer joints" nor "cocktail lounges" to be found in Lincoln. It opened as the Bon Ton Lunch in 1924, when Prohibition was the law of the land. Sam Veltman was the Lunch's initial proprietor. He was later joined by Kenneth Fogg. The man most remembered through the years, however, is John Goode, who served as cook/ bartender/manager and was "five feet wide and six feet tall." Most every Friday, fondly recalls Kenwood Boyington again, John would steam up a bushel of soft shell clams and give them away to the Bon Ton's assembled multitudes.

For those who did patronize the Bon Ton there were good times and good food. In the early 1950s John and Polly Swanson used to motor down from Millinocket in John's Nash Ambassador: "In Millinocket the sidewalks were rolled up early, so we'd come to Lincoln and the Bon Ton after a dance," smiles John.

In 1949 Francis "Dick" Walsh took over the proprietorship of the Bon Ton. He ran it an even dozen years, until a combination of ill health and a desire to move on caused him to put what had become a landmark on the market in 1961. The only taker, however, was Smart's Farm Supply, located next door at 57 Main Street. Smart's, though, had no interest in running a restaurant: they wanted the space to expand. The result: the Bon Ton became history. On its former site there is today still the expanded Smart's, now called Smart's True Value Hardware.

TO SUIT YOUR TASTE

THE BON TON RESTAURANT

Quality Food--Prices Right

We Now Have a Private

Dining Room for Special Parties

SWift 4-8965   59 Main Street

Lincoln, Maine

Ad, 1959, PINE NEEDLES, the yearbook of Mattanawcook Academy, Lincoln. In business from 1924 to 1961, the Bon Ton was a fixture on Lincoln's Main Street – which was also Route 2, Maine's major east-west artery until I-95 came along – for close to four decades. Legend has it that no less a personage than the Bambino, Babe Ruth, partook of the Bon Ton's hospitality on a visit through town one day in 1938.

CLARKE'S NORMANDIE
SCARBOROUGH

Scarborough, just south of Portland, has long been favored with a supply of roadside eateries, especially along coastal U.S. Route 1. What became Clarke's Normandie was one of the very first. It was begun by partners Earl Bennett and Cliff Leary circa 1925 and dubbed – why not? – the Earlcliff. At first take-out only, the duo's hot dogs, fried clams, and home-made ice cream sold so well that it soon became necessary to add an inside dining room.

By 1929 Earl had bought out Cliff. The Earlcliff became the Benway. Another name change, to Dunsboro Farms, came in the early 1930s. Finally, circa 1938, the name "Clarke's Normandie" appeared, the result of Ernest and Mildred Clarke becoming the new proud proprietors. Two years later, in 1940, in a step well ahead of its time, the Clarkes hired a Hindu chef, "Mr. Mohammed Karim," formerly of Swampscott, Massachusetts. Ads promised "Visit our place once, try our outstanding food, then you, like so many others, will become regular patrons."

The restaurant operated as Clarke's Normandie until 1951. It then became the Holiday Inn (no relation to *the* Holiday Inn). It is today occupied by an amusement game distributor, Oliver Vending and Music Systems, and appears not unlike it did in its restaurant days of old.

Postcard view, circa 1940. "Why not drive out to the Normandie for your Sunday Dinner?" asked a May 1940 ad.

CLARKE'S **NORMANDIE** — WEST SCARBORO, MAINE

ROUTE I AT DUNSTON CORNER, BETWEEN BIDDEFORD AND PORTLAND

COLE'S DINING ROOM
CHINA

Excellent service, top grade fare, and "coffee so hot you'd burn your fingers" on the cup. That's what made Cole's Dining Room what it was, recounts Muriel Adams. And "what it was" was one of the very best places to enjoy a meal in all of central Maine in the 1930s and into the mid-forties. Cole's was built by Muriel's uncle, William "Will" Cole, in 1932-1933. Tourist cabins – eight of them – came first. Then came the hip-roofed delight pictured here. Cole was a native of New Brunswick, Canada. For a time he owned and operated a grocery store on the shores of China Lake but, as Muriel phrases it, "He saw a better business opportunity with a restaurant."

Muriel waitressed at "Uncle Will's" from 1939 until 1944.

She recalls that Sunday, not surprisingly, was the *big* day. Steak, roast turkey, or Cole's renowned New England boiled dinner. The choice was yours. "We used to have a doctor and his wife who would drive over from Laconia, New Hampshire." And what would they always have? "The boiled dinner. Absolutely."

William Cole passed away in 1944. His former place became the Lakeview Dining Room through the 1950s and the early 1960s. It then became the Candlewood, with Muriel and her husband Albert the pride-filled proprietors. They ran it until 1997. "We made every effort to change nothing," Muriel reflected in a November 1999 interview at her home in China. You knew it was a very special reflection.

Postcard view, circa 1940. Courtesy of Peter D. Bachelder, Ellsworth. Muriel Adams sold Candlewood, which is located on U.S. Route 202, to Alan and Judy Gilman in 1997. They, it's gratifying to say, have continued on in the very same "Why change a good thing?" fashion.

Colonial Maid Restaurant   Brunswick, Me.

Brunswick-Bath Highway U.S. 1.

Postcard view, circa 1950. Courtesy Peter D. Bachelder, Ellsworth. The site of the Colonial Maid, at the junction of Bath Road and Thomas Point Road, is now occupied by a laundromat.

THE COLONIAL MAID
BRUNSWICK

The Colonial Maid opened in 1947. On June 14th. Kiddies got a free cone. There were 16 flavors from which to choose. Plus several gallons of ice cream were given away as door prizes. "Four Brunswick and Bath people were among the winners," noted *The Brunswick Record*.

Steak, pork chops, lamb chops, "the best fried clams," and lobster rolls - at 40¢ each - were also on the bill. Southern fried chicken was soon added.

The Colonial Maid's proprietor was Bath-native Daniel Poulos. Just out of the Army, he was joined by his parents and other relatives. "It was a family thing," he recounted in an October 1999 conversation. The name "Colonial Maid"

came about because Daniel's sister was, again per Daniel, "kind of an artist and she had drawn a silhouette of a young maiden."

The Colonial Maid, open from late May until autumn, operated for a solid decade and a half until commercial growth in the Cook's Corner section of Brunswick necessitated widening the King's Turnpike (now Bath Road) portion of old U.S. Route 1. The Colonial Maid was a casualty. All these years later Daniel Poulos, still living in Bath, gets upset at what the state did. "I don't want to talk about it," he sums up.

DOWE'S DINER
SOUTH CHINA

Barbara (Dowe) Poulin gets sentimental when she talks about Dowe's Diner. And well she should: she spent more than a fair share of her growing-up years at the diner. Her children, in turn, then spent more than a fair share of their's.

Barbara's dad, veteran eatery proprietor Edmund "Ed" Dowe, purchased the diner in 1946. It had been sitting idle, just east of Augusta on Route 17 near the Togus Veterans' Hospital. Ed had the diner moved the 20 or so miles to his hometown of South China, refurbished it, and called it Dowe's Diner.

"It (the diner) was a very well-known eating place, especially for the clams, fried in batter," reminisces Barbara. "The locals would come in for coffee, 'tall tales' and friendly games of cribbage." Ed, Barbara's mother Alice, and Barbara all worked at Dowe's. So did Barbara's four sisters. "It was family," Barbara says simply.

Photo, circa 1955. Courtesy of Barbara Poulin, South China.

Dowe's Diner as it appeared in an "on the road" shot taken in the mid-1950s. The road you see is Route 3 before it was re-routed. Now it's just plain Village Street. And most everything pictured is gone. Photo courtesy of Barbara Poulin, South China.

Here's Barbara as she looked in a circa 1954 snapshot. "This is me at the grill. My dad made the pastries and doughnuts and pies seen in the foreground. He made all kinds of pies. And they were thick. They weren't skinny little pies." Photo courtesy of Barbara Poulin, South China.

In the 1950s and 1960s, with children of her own, Barbara continued to work at the diner. It became almost a second home for all of them. Years later, in fact, Barbara's son Craig took pen in hand to express what Dowe's Diner had meant to him:

> There was no place found
> In this little town
> Where friendship was finer
> And for years you were found
> Til at last it closed down
> At the haven we knew as "the Diner."
>
> Though you never got rich
> And didn't gain fame
> Why, it probably even grew old
> What it allowed you to give
> To us kids growing up
> Were things many times better than gold.

The diner as a viable business operation began to wane in the mid-1960s. "He (her dad) was tired from all the work; all the hours," recalls Barbara. In 1968 Ed sold the diner to his daughter (and Barbara's sister) Gloria and her husband, Joe Pinnette. It closed in 1972, and was demolished several years later.

EDGAR'S BIDDEFORD

You have to admire Alexander Edgar. Subtle he was not. To claim to be "sanitary" was a not uncommon marketing strategy in the decades of not so long ago. To state, however, that the entirety of your fellow eatery proprietors – and Edgar was but one of 13 restaurateurs in Biddeford at the time – oversaw "Dyspeptic (Dyspepsia = 'difficult and painful digestion') Factories" was quite another matter.

Alexander Edgar ran Edgar's from 1910 until 1915…when he abandoned the food service industry and became a machinist.

FRANK CONROY'S LUNCH
SANFORD

Frank Conroy and his brother Jack were early 20th Century lunch wagon moguls. They were seemingly everywhere in southern Maine in the years 1914 to 1934 (see photo caption on the facing page). The result: it's difficult to document their activities with any degree of real accuracy. For example, you can't miss the "1914" written atop the photo postcard featured here. On the back of the card it reads "Frank Conroy/ Sanford." Yet business directory listings of the day do not show Frank's arrival in Sanford until 1920 or 1921. That's when he ran a lunch wagon on Washington Street. By 1924 the Conroys had doubled their presence in Sanford, but it was Jack who got star billing: both lunch wagons were called "Jack's Lunch." One was located at 35½ High Street and was managed by Frank. The other, at 7 School Street, lists Jack as the man in charge. By 1927 the brothers were back to one address, 7 School, with Jack the proprietor, but Frank the manager; the on-the-scene operator. By 1932 (there were no Sanford business directories published between 1927 and 1932) the brothers were gone. Lunch in Sanford would never be the same.

Photo postcard, 1914 (?). Courtesy of Maine Historic Preservation Commission, Augusta. From Sanford to Boothbay Harbor and Bath to Portland and Old Orchard, Frank Conroy and his brother Jack served up lunch wagon lunches galore.

Photo, circa 1925. Courtesy of Maine Historic Preservation Commission, Augusta. In addition to Bath and Sanford, John Conroy also, at one time or another, had lunch carts in operation in Boothbay Harbor, Old Orchard Beach, and Portland. He passed away, at age 72, in East Hampden, Maine in 1962.

JACK'S LUNCH
BATH

This dandy lunch wagon arrived in Bath circa 1916. Its address was 89-91 Centre Street. It began as Stacy Brothers' Lunch. Then it was Bill's Lunch ("Good Food/ Good Service/Moderate Prices/Try Us"). "Jack," John J. Conroy, took over in 1923. Jack was far from a stranger to the food service industry: his father, John E. Conroy, had been a lunch cart man in both Lynn, Massachusetts and his home town of Bangor. And father and son had teamed up to run the Star Restaurant at 22-24 Front Street in Bath from 1917 to 1920. Then there was Jack and his brother Frank's ventures in Sanford (see facing page).

Jack's sported but ten stools and no booths. It was open, recalls Jack's son Donald, from 4:00 PM until 1:00 or 2:00 AM and was noted for its sandwiches and its pies.

Especially the pies: Jack's wife, Annie, and mother, Lettie, did the baking and, again recalls Donald, are remembered as being real good at it.

Along about 1934, Jack began to lose interest in his lunch. It seems one of his employees liked to bum cigarettes, causing Jack to install a cigarette vending machine. Then in its infancy, the machine proved such a hit that Jack set up his own vending operation. He sold the diner, in 1935, to better focus on this new business.

After Jack's departure his cart was utilized as a lunch by three additional proprietors. In the name of Urban Renewal, however, the cart was demolished in 1950. Its former site is now occupied by a parking lot.

KEN & GERRY'S DINNER
KITTERY

"As a kid everybody went there. We all got a kick out of going in one door and out the other." That's what 63-year old James Cole recalls when he thinks of Ken's (nee Ken & Gerry's) Diner. That and the diner's small size. "It had about eight-to-ten stools and a number of little two-seater tables. It was," chuckles Jim, "nothing you'd have a ten-course meal at."

Ken Quintal began in the diner business in 1936, operating Ken's Diner at 95 Vaughn Street in Portsmouth, and then Ken's Cafe at 141 Vaughn, also in Portsmouth. In 1940 Ken made the big move across the Piscataqua to Kittery and Maine where he appears to have taken over a shortlived operation known as Happy's Diner, changing its name to Ken & Gerry's. "Gerry" was his wife Geraldine.

Ken & Gerry's was located right downtown - yes, there really is a downtown Kittery - at 51 Wallingford Square. He couldn't have picked a better time to be where he was. With World War II on the horizon the Portsmouth Navy Yard (actually in Kittery and very near Wallingford Square) was mushrooming both in size and mouths to feed.

"Ken & Gerry's" became just "Ken's" in 1947. Either by himself or in concert with his wife, though, Ken was a popular guy. "Everybody liked him," remembers 73-year old Gordon Cutten. "He didn't seem to ever get mad. He was always telling stories. Always kidding. Always jovial."

Gordon also recalls, however, that Ken's health failed him in the early 1960s. He was forced to close his namesake eatery. That was 1963. Soon thereafter the diner was demolished to make way for an addition to the Kittery branch of the First National Bank of Portland.

Ad, 1945, THE RANGER'S LOG, yearbook of R.W. Traip Academy, Kittery. Courtesy of R.W. Traip Academy, Kittery. "It (the diner) was nothing you'd have a ten-course meal at."

KEN & GERRY'S DINER

"The food is good. The prices right."

Fast and Efficient Service

Photo, circa 1950. Courtesy of Mrs. Dana Cheney, Monticello. The Miss Aroostook stood at 9 Bangor Street/Union Square, just about where the Dallas Henderson State Farm agency is now.

MISS AROOSTOOK HOULTON

Photo, circa 1950. Courtesy of Mrs. Dana Cheney, Monticello

The Miss Aroostook was a "Worcester," manufactured by the Worcester Lunch Car Company, of Worcester, Massachusetts, and by all accounts it was a beauty. Bright blue and yellow on the outside; sparkling and shiny and adorned with a marble counter on the inside. It was started up on Monday, November 24, 1947, was open seven days a week from 5:00 AM to midnight, featured a Rockola jukebox, and promised full course meals, short order lunches, and special Sunday dinners.

The diner lived up to its promises. "A good place to stop. Good coffee, good doughnuts, cheerful service." That's how long-time resident Bruce Burnham remembers the Miss Aroostook. Mary Suitter, also a long-time Houltonite, is even more emphatic. "Damned good food" are her words.

The Miss Aroostook's initial proprietor was Glen Philbrick, who described himself as "the rotund owner." In 1959 he sold to Dana Cheney. Dana, however, also owned Dana's Food Store in Houlton. Eventually trying to run both endeavors proved to be too much. Dana closed the diner circa 1972.

All these years later part of the Miss Aroostook yet exists. It is attached to the side of a presently-closed bar, grill and pool hall, formerly known as Mumm's, located at 142 Military Road, Houlton. What remains, however, looks nothing at all like what you see here.

Ad, August 1957, HOULTON HAS ITS 150th BIRTHDAY SOUVENIR PROGRAM.

Postcard view, circa 1938. Courtesy of Peter D. Bachelder, Ellsworth

T GROUND
WELCHVILLE (OXFORD)

Welchville is that section of Oxford where Routes 26 and 121 come together. It's a seldom-used name nowadays. But Bernice "Bee" (Paine) Merrill knows Welchville. And the building pictured here. "I worked there as a waitress for a short time after high school. That would've been 1941 or '42." Bee's memories are good ones, too: she worked right alongside her high school friend, Eleanor "Ellie" (Fortier) Pulkkinen. They waitressed together.

The building that Bee and Ellie recall began as Grant's Tea Room, opened by Sherm and Sadie Grant circa 1930. The postcard photo shown here is most likely from 1938 or so, with "T Ground" a way of saying "tea room." In 1940 Grant's became Watson's; Earle and Mabel Watson, proprietors. Bee recalls them as "nice people." She also recalls – and smiles a big smile – that Earle and Mabel would some-times drive to Portland for supplies and she and Ellie would partake of some of Mabel's just-made pie for lunch. "Oh, yes, they had good pies."

Ellie's husband, Sulo, has a recollection of Watson's, too. One a little more somber than partaking of pie. "I," he says, "was out riding around one day back in 1941 with my brother Carl and our friend Bud Green when we went in there (Watson's) to get coffee and a hamburger and play the jukebox. And then all of a sudden it came over the radio that the Japanese had attacked Pearl Harbor. It was a shock. It was like a death in the family."

In 1943 Earle Watson joined the war effort and took a job in the shipyard in South Portland. Watson's was closed. Not long thereafter it was demolished. On the site today are the offices of a trucking company.

Bee and her boyfriend Jim's
1936 Ford at Watson's, 1941

Bee by Jim's car at Watsons

1941

"They had tables. It wasn't a big place. And I don't ever recall a big crowd in there at any one time. I don't think it was too prosperous."

Bernice "Bee" Merrill

1941

Bee + Ellie at Watsons

Bee and Ellie and
others in front of
Watson's, 1941

Bee and Ellie and
Jim's Ford, 1941

Watsons Tea Room

"I remember one breakfast where I waited on a man and he had a softboiled egg and Ellie and I served it in a little sauce dish and he was a little irritated that it wasn't served in an egg cup."

Bernice "Bee" Merrill

"They sold to local people who'd stop for gas. They sold to tourists going through. There weren't a lot of other eating places around."

Eleanor "Ellie" Pulkkinen

U-WANTA LUNCH
MONTICELLO

U-Wanta Lunch was a fine example of what I think of as "suggestive" wording. Not suggestive in a sexual manner; suggestive in the true sense of the word: to suggest, or almost command, a certain course of action. Maine entrepreneurs, especially, seemed to have delighted in such names. There's been Dun-Romin Cabins (Skowhegan), Far-Enuf Tourist Home (Skowhegan), Idle-A-While (Sullivan), Linger-A-While Lunch (Harrington), Ramble Inn (Bath; see page 55), Stumble Inn Cabins (Cape Neddick), Tarry-A-While (West Scarborough). And who could forget the numerous places named Dew Drop Inn?

Back to U-Wanta. "It was a great place to eat. They had tables set all around the porch and a big dining room." That's how Carlton Brewer, who's lived in the area his entire life, describes Monticello's contribution to roadside restaurants. He also recalls it being known as Ramsey's Lunch. Makes sense: the place was owned by Annie and Ben Ramsey. The couple had cabins, too. Business, mostly from passing tourists and road-building crews, was good.

U-Wanta/Ramsey's operated from 1933 to 1942. There is now a grassy field where the restaurant and cabins, on U. S. Route 1 a mile south of the post office, once stood.

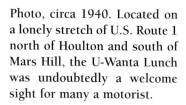

Photo, circa 1940. Located on a lonely stretch of U.S. Route 1 north of Houlton and south of Mars Hill, the U-Wanta Lunch was undoubtedly a welcome sight for many a motorist.

"U-WANTA LUNCH"
MONTICELLO, ME.

WEDGEMERE MOTOR INN, OGUNQUIT, ME. M. J. GLEASON, PROP.

OPEN YEAR ROUND.

Postcard view, circa 1932, and ad from *Friends Along the Road* magazine, August 1928.

WEDGEMERE
OGUNQUIT

Wedgemere harks back to quieter days in the Ogunquit-Wells' coastal area of southern Maine. Lifelong resident Doris (Brown) Clogston, 81, recalls those days well: "This was always a tourist place, along Route 1, the Coast Road. On July the Fourth (and thereafter) the roads would be packed with tourists' cars. Then, come Labor Day, it was almost like they were all wiped off the map. And we went back to knowing everybody that was there."

Wedgemere opened in 1924, with George and Marie Gleason at the helm. Overnight accommodations were offered. So were meals, with Marie doing the cooking. It's those meals that are remembered. "Excellent," "Prepared the way they should be," and "Served right" are words that are used. As Doris sums up: "I think people liked her (Marie's) cooking."

George passed away circa 1927. Marie then ran things on her own until 1938 when she sold to sisters Clara and Mary Richardson. They changed the name to Richardson's Ogunquit Inn. A later name change, to Poor Richard's Pub, was made in the late 1960s. In the late 1980s the building, wrap-around-porch and all, was demolished. On the site there is now the Ocean Towers Resort Hotel.

THE WIGWAM
MILFORD

The Wigwam opened in 1927-1928 with Maude and George Martin doing both the owning and the operating. "It (the restaurant) was just a small, little place…a few tables and a place where she (Maude) cooked," recalls 84-year old Ruby Hildreth, who grew up nearby. Hot dogs and hamburgers and the like were the daily fare. But Maude would have specials, too. Pot roast is one that comes to Ruby's mind. Chicken dinners were another specialty. Then there were pies, too, of course. And, in the truest sense of "real home cooking," Maude baked her pies at home.

The Wigwam did an okay business for most of its years. "At that time," ventures Ruby, "there used to be a lot of truckers going by" on Route 2, the "Pine Tree Trail," and a lot of them would stop and eat.

George, who was also a state legislator, died circa 1937. Maude "run it more or less on her own," recalls Ruby, until she, too, died, in 1940 or 1941. No one else bothered to keep George and Maude's creation in operation. It was eventually demolished. On the site today is the Milford Motel.

Ad, *Motoring Thru Maine* booklet, circa 1936. George and Maude knew it: there's magic in those words "real old fashioned home cooking."

THE WIGWAM CAMPS

On "Pine Tree Trail"   Route 2   MILFORD, MAINE
14 Miles North of Bangor   MRS. GEO. E. MARTIN, Prop.
"HOSPITAL CLEAN" cabins of better kind, among shady pines, with sun-rooms overlooking Penobscot River. Private flushes, baths, both tub and shower.   Real old fashioned home cooking.
Tel. Oldtown 2157

Photograph, circa 1935. Courtesy of Maine Historic Preservation Commission, Augusta. It would most likely be deemed politically incorrect in this day and age, but the name "Wigwam" no doubt sounded inviting, perhaps even exotic, to Maude and George Martin away back in 1927-1928.

Photo, circa 1947. Courtesy of Alice Clark, Palm Springs, Florida. They loved "Andy's chicken."

Postcard view, circa 1948.

THE WILLOWS
ELLSWORTH

Sometimes too much business can be a problem. Ask Alice Clark. She and her husband Andrew ("Andy") had owned/operated the Sun Diner on the Bar Harbor road in Ellsworth. In 1946, though, they sold it. "The business had become so big and we were open 18 hours a day," recalls Alice. "My husband had arthritis and it was just too much."

Next stop was the Willows, an already-in-existence cabin and small eatery complex on the Bangor road (Route 1A) that Alice and Andy purchased that same year. The couple's intent was to serve meals to only their overnight cabin customers. Their former Sun patrons, however, had other plans. They drove on out to the Willows almost en masse. "My husband was a natural born cook," smiles Alice. Andy's fried chicken was especially popular. The eatery, dubbed "Andy's Diner," was soon abandoned in favor of a much larger facility across the road. The result was, again, too much work and too many hours. "I never worked so hard or had so much fun doing it," laughs Alice today. The couple, both with health problems, sold the Willows and moved to Florida in 1950. Andy passed away in 1977. The couple's former Sun Diner now serves as a video store. The Willows has long since been torn down.

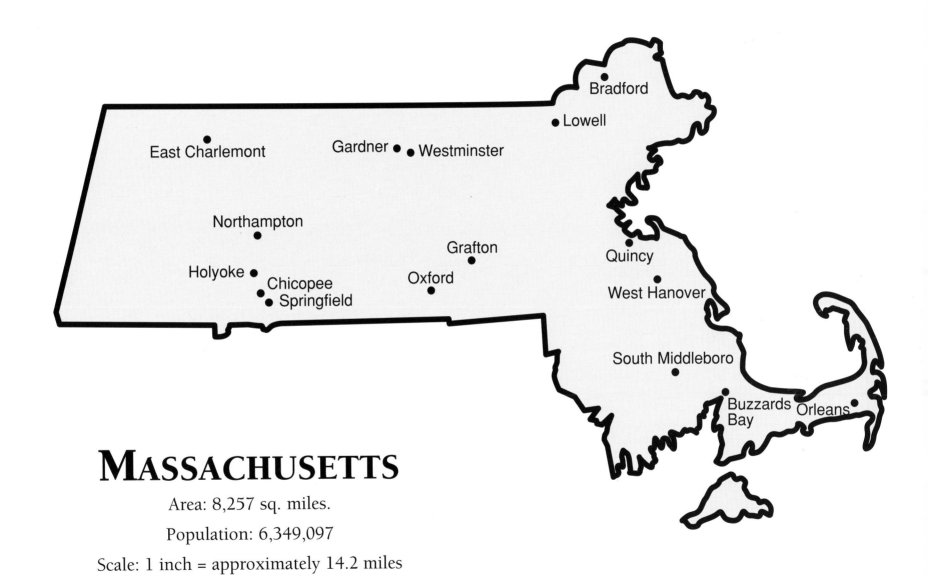

East Charlemont

Gardner • Westminster

Bradford

Lowell

Northampton

Grafton

Holyoke
Chicopee
Springfield

Oxford

Quincy

West Hanover

South Middleboro

Buzzards
Bay

Orleans

MASSACHUSETTS

Area: 8,257 sq. miles.

Population: 6,349,097

Scale: 1 inch = approximately 14.2 miles

AL'S LUNCH
LOWELL

There are some stories that are probably best left untold. Al's Lunch is one of them. The photo shown here is a part of the prestigious Locks and Canals Collection, over 4,000 photographs that chronicle Lowell's history from the late 1870s to the 1940s. The date of the photo, according to official Locks and Canals records, is April 23, 1935. Even the street location is given, right there on the photo.

With the above knowledge in hand I breezed into Lowell on what would appear to be an easy assignment. That's when the troubles began. To begin with, LOWELL CITY DIRECTORY listings fail to *ever* show an Al's Lunch. Al's Taxi; Al's Filling Station; Al's Diner (at a location many blocks from this photo and not in operation until 1946): yes. Al's Lunch: no. City Hall records – and the people at City Hall sure did their best – show a Dad's Lunch in the vicinity, but no Al's. And numerous conversations with old-timers around town produced nothing but conflicting memories. At the Club Passe-Temps (near the site in what was called "Little Canada") I spoke with gentlemen who recalled Al's as being gone by 1938 ("They knocked it down in 1936, 1937 or maybe after the Hurricane of 1938"); still in business through the 1940s ("Breakfast was their big meal: bacon and eggs or pancakes."); there in the early 1950s ("I recall it being there. It was abandoned when I remember it, in the early 1950s.") Interested parties – and everyone was interested – came up with Al's last name as Brochette, Defresne, DuFour, and Hebert. None checked out.

So, what do we know for sure? That Al's Lunch was there, right over the Aiken Street Bridge, where the entrance to the parking lot for Albert H. Notini & Sons is now. That Al's Lunch was there. And that now it's not.

A FIVE-DINER TOWN

While Lowell has lost Al's Lunch it's still a five-diner town… and how many of those can you think of? There's Arthur's Paradise (112 Bridge Street), the Club Diner ("Open Day and Night Since '38") at 145 Dutton Street, the Owl Diner at 244 Appleton Street, Trolley Stop Pizzaria Plus at 984 Gorham Street, and (remodeled and added-onto) Elliot's Famous Hot Dogs at 37 Elliot Street. In addition there's Danas, a since-1914 confectionary/soda fountain at 62-66 Gorham Street that's like stepping back almost nine decades. It's a delight.

CHEEVER ST.

AIKEN ST.

Photo, April 23, 1935. Courtesy of UMass Lowell Center for Lowell History. What remains from this photo is the bridge grillwork shown on the right and City Hall's arching spire in the background left. Everything else has been leveled and replaced.

Photo, June 1931. Courtesy of the Trustees of Haverhill Public Library, Haverhill.
Standing proud is Al on the left and chief cook Ray Cummings on the right.

AL'S WARD 7 DINER
BRADFORD (HAVERHILL)

Alvin "Al" Kneeland had been around the block a time or two before he opened this gem of a diner in the Bradford section of Haverhill in early June 1931. A native of Georgetown (Massachusetts), Kneeland had considerable experience as a shoemaker in Haverhill's numerous shoe factories. He'd owned and operated a pair of diners, too. Al's Ward 7 was his crowning achievement. It was a brand new Ward & Dickinson (See page 95.). Al named his endeavor the "Ward 7" because, when Bradford was merged into Haverhill in 1897, it became the city's seventh ward. Al's Ward 7 replaced an earlier diner (you can just make out part of the earlier diner on the right) at the same address, 47 South Main Street. The earlier model had been in service since 1923 and had been known first as Arthur's Lunch (Arthur A. Demarais, proprietor) and then as Gilmore's Lunch (James J. Gilmore, proprietor).

The photo included here was taken to honor the diner's opening. Underneath the photo, which ran in the June 7, 1931 edition of *The Haverhill Sunday Record*, there was quite the write-up. It read:

> The cool comfortable atmosphere of the diner, its up-to-the-minute fittings and equipment, combined with the very delicious home-cooked foods served in an appetizing manner by 'Al' Kneeland and Ray Cummings, are some of the many reasons responsible for the rapidly increasing list of satisfied customers.
>
> The interior of the Ward and Dickinson, the only car of its kind in this city, is finished in harmonizing green and ivory of a most attractive shade, and there are two booths for special parties near the entrance as well as a long marble topped bar extending along the center of the car, making a total seating capacity of 20 persons. The electric dish washing machine is an exclusive feature of the Ward 7 diner and a large Kelvinator refrigerator keeps food perfectly.
>
> Grilled sandwiches are a specialty of the Ward 7 diner, and home cooked foods and pastries are a large drawing card. Coffee is served with plenty of rich cream and special dinners and suppers are featured every day.

Whew! There's actually more, too. Suffice it to say that Al's Ward 7 was the place to be.

Alvin Kneeland ran his diner until 1937. He then appears to have retired. His former diner thereafter led a checkered open/closed existence into the 1950s. It was Duffy's Lunch (Clement P. DuFresne, proprietor) in the early 1950s. Then it was Sunny's Diner (John Melia, proprietor) for a year or so. It was, most likely, demolished in the late fifties. On its old site there is now a Wendy's.

P.S. If you grew up in the Boston area in the 1950s you will probably remember Eileen Kneeland, star of the early fifties' show, THE LADY OF THE BOOKSHELF, over WBZ-TV. Eileen Kneeland was Al's daughter.

Photo, circa 1952. Courtesy of Arvo Niemi, Westminster. Arvo had a contract with Trailways in the early 1950s. Eight busses would stop – so passengers could eat – each day during the week. On weekends that count doubled, to 16. "The bus would stop," Arvo beams, "and they (the passengers) would swarm in. It was terrific business."

CAPE ANN DINER
WESTMINSTER

"Every day someone would ask me where to eat," states Arvo Niemi, remembering back to when he operated a Mobilgas station on busy Route 2 (the old Route 2) in Westminster in the days after World War II. So he thought: "Why not a dining car?" and proceeded to discuss the idea with the Worcester Lunch Car Company. Arvo liked Worcester Lunch Car because he liked the idea that he could watch his diner being made. He was, however, shocked at the price. "They told me they could build one (a diner) that would accommodate 34 people for $20,000." Heck, he reflects, "At that time you could buy a nice two-bedroom home for $7,500."

Arvo ended up settling for a used (just barely used; it was but nine months old) diner. Here's how it happened: a man from Gloucester purchased a Worcester; had it set up in Gloucester; named it the Cape Ann (Gloucester is on Cape Ann); then, almost immediately, found it to be too small for his needs. Arvo jumped in, bought the infant diner (for $15,500 for the same model that would have cost him $20,000 brand new), and had it moved to a site in Westminster. "It (the move) was something," well recalls Arvo. "We started at midnight and the flatbed truck and diner were so big we had to trim tree branches as we went.

It took us to 3:00 the next afternoon to get to Westminster. There was a crowd waiting."

The diner opened June 8, 1948. Instead of calling it "Arvo's Grill" or the like, Arvo kept the "Cape Ann" name. "I'd spent $840.00 for the move," explains the Fitchburg native, "and the name ("Cape Ann") was already (baked) in the porcelain panels and it would have cost to get all new panels." Besides, he laughs, "People going east would see the name and think they were near the ocean and they'd say 'Let's stop and eat.' Then I'd tell 'em they were 50 miles from the ocean and they'd laugh and eat anyway."

In 1956 Arvo sold his diner and bought the Chetwood Inn (touted as "New England's Finest Restaurant") in neighboring Templeton. Eventually, however, the new by-pass Route 2 killed off much of the Chetwood's trade, and Arvo came home to the Cape Ann, re-purchasing it in 1968. Even the diner's business, though, was well down from its pre-bypass days. In 1972 Arvo moved his diner back from the old highway, selling the frontage property to Cumberland Farms. He then sold off the diner's insides and converted half of it into a barber shop and half into a reality office. That, too, though, became more trouble than it was worth after a time. In 1984 Arvo sold the diner and the land it was on to the local VFW. They proceeded to level everything to add to the size of their parking lot.

Today Arvo, 83, lives in Westminster half the year and in Lake Worth, Florida the other half. I asked him if he missed the diner. He replied "Well, yes, I miss it. When I go by (where it used to be) I always picture the diner there."

Photo, March 1968. Courtesy of Arvo Niemi, Westminster. Arvo with his wife Ellen. "She liked to come down and eat lunch," reminisces Arvo. "She especially liked our fish: fried clams, scallops, halibut. That was her favorite: halibut."

HI-HAT CAFE
GARDNER

It was 1927. The Babe blasted his 60 home runs. "Lucky Lindy" crossed the Atlantic in his Spirit of St. Louis. And 33-year old Italian immigrant Amedeo Sbrega (often spelled Sbiga) opened a confectionary shop in Gardner, Massachusetts. Known as "The Chair City," Gardner could easily have then been "The Sweet City" as well: Amedeo's shop was one of 21 sweet and/or ice cream shops in operation in the north central Massachusetts city at the time.

Amedeo – nicknamed "Shorty" because he was far from tall – operated his confectionary until 1937, when he blossomed the operation into a full-scale cafe he named the Hi-Hat.

Sure, there were still sweets to be had, but there was also pot roast, liver and onions, and roast beef, "and don't forget spaghetti," laughs daughter-in-law Edith Sbrega when asked about the Hi-Hat's best known dishes.

Shorty, with help from his son John, operated his cafe through the 1940s and 1950s. In 1960 he sold the Hi-Hat. Instead of retiring, however, he started anew, operating the Main Street Coffee Shop at 132 Main Street until his death, at age 75, in January 1971. Meanwhile the Hi-Hat, under various proprietors, continued until 1977. Its 124 Main address then saw several eating / drinking establishments come and go until area-native Joanne LeBlanc purchased the property in 1988 and named it Joanne's Pub. Since then, with live bands on weekends and such basics as steamed hot dogs, roast beef and ham, and cheese bulkies all week long, Joanne has resurrected the essence of Shorty Sbrega's old Hi-Hat Cafe. (P.S. If you visit, make it a double-play day by also stopping in at Skip's Blue Moon Diner, a delightful 1949 Worcester located just up the block at 102 Main.).

Photo, summer 1947. Courtesy of Edith Sbrega and Joanne LeBlanc, both Gardner. Left-to-right there's Shorty's wife, Alice; Shorty's niece, Sonia; Shorty; Shorty's sister-in-law, Emily…and Shorty's automobile, a 1937 Chevrolet.

IN-WEE-GO
SMITH'S FERRY (HOLYOKE)

There are no known photos of the In-Wee-Go. Too bad: it sounds like it was a neat place. Bob Schwobe, who ate there two or three times a week in the early 1960s, was so fond of it he even sat down and drew me a sketch of the building's floor plan.

The In-Wee-Go sprang up in 1948. Located in the Smith's Ferry section of Holyoke on busy U.S. Route 5, the In-Wee-Go was assured of a steady flow of business. To aid that flow the In featured carhops. "You'd pull up and there'd be a thin, shapely girl in short shorts and a tight shirt," fondly recalls lifelong Holyoke resident Don Breen. "The waitress was their advertising." Don, who's 73 and whose memories are circa 1950, remembers the In's foot-long hot dogs. Bob Schwobe, who's 67 and whose memories are circa 1962, also recalls the hot dogs but he generally went with the special of the day. "I don't like hot dogs," he says. "But meatloaf. Hamburg steak. Franks & beans. I'd see what the special was and I'd usually eat that." Regardless of what he ate Bob recalls that "It was good and generous. More than you'd get at a Howard Johnson's. Absolutely! It was not portion control." By 1967, however the In-Wee-Go was gone, demolished to make way for the construction of the building, a union hall, that's still there today.

Matchbook cover, circa 1950. The "Mel's" is a mystery. Not one of the half-dozen people I spoke with ever knew the In-Wee-Go as "Mel's," and no "Mel's" ever appears in any business listings. Even Paul Graves, head of the Holyoke Public Library's excellent History Room, drew a blank. "I'm up in the air," he admitted.

Most people get a kick out of old menus because of the "bargain" prices. A fried clam dinner for $1.00 or a slice of pineapple cream pie for 15¢

does have a certain ring to it. But menu artwork - the designs and illustrations that gave the menu its "feel" – can have appeal, too. Jack August's menu is a favorite of mine.

Menus, all circa 1945

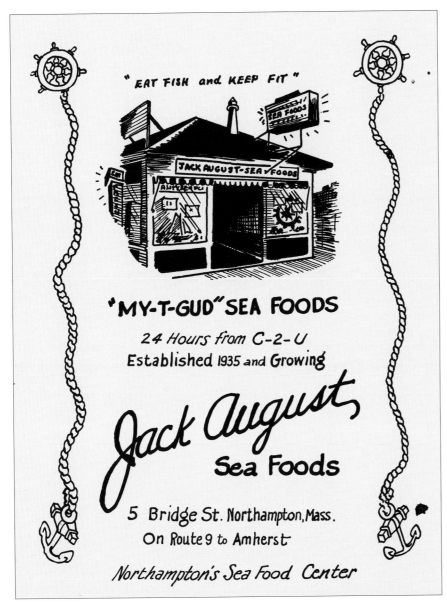

"EAT FISH and KEEP FIT"

"MY-T-GUD" SEA FOODS

24 Hours from C-2-U
Established 1935 and Growing

Jack August
Sea Foods

5 Bridge St. Northampton, Mass.
On Route 9 to Amherst

Northampton's Sea Food Center

Menu, circa 1945

A message from Jack on his menu's inside front cover

Have you found anything you like? **NO?** Ask the Waitress for **JACK'S SUGGESTION** "You'll like it!"

JACK AUGUST NORTHAMPTON

Jack August began as a from-the-back-seat-of-his-car purveyor of meat in Northampton in the early 1930s. He added fish – on Fridays only – at his customers' request. Once "into" fish, Jack really got into fish. He made certain he carried only fish that was the very freshest; what he dubbed "The top of the catch." (As each fisherman's catch is hauled aboard, the newest is stacked atop the others: it's "The top of the catch.").

Jack graduated to his own market – selling fish only – in 1935. Before long customers were asking him to cook the fish for them, too. Jack, described by his daughter Rita as a "jolly fat man" ("He loved people and people loved him."), obliged. Several expansions later, Jack August's was a full-fledged restaurant serving fish and only fish. No meat. No beer. No wine. No liquor.

Jack, with considerable help from his wife Eva, operated the restaurant until 1968. Various proprietors, some family/some not, then ran the venerable eatery until it closed in 1994. It is now, under entirely different ownership, operated as the Paradise City Tavern.

LAKE RIPPLE CAFE
GRAFTON

"It's always been there," said 86-year old Chester Zaleski when I asked him about the Lake Ripple Cafe. Chester's about right. The Cafe appears to go back to 1928 or 1929 when Henry and Elmira Neiger opened their Neiger's Inn on Worcester Street near Lake Ripple. A circa 1930 post-card shows Neiger's as a small wooden-frame structure replete with signs advertising coffee, Velvet brand ice cream, cold soft drinks, sandwiches (chicken, ham, west-ern, others), and homemade pies and cake. A pair of gas pumps stood ready... with gas at 17¢ the gallon.

Neiger's folded sometime in the mid-1930s, with a man named Eugene Chatigny taking over and enlarging the operation. Eugene also changed the restaurant's name to the Lake Ripple Lunch.

Almost seven decades later the Lake Ripple – It became the Lake Ripple *Restaurant* in 1966 – remains a favorite. There's still coffee, ice cream, and sandwiches, plus, under the ownership of Jerry Fleming and family, such specials as prime rib and seafood.

Postcard view, circa 1940. Today's Lake Ripple looks much the same. The big differ-ence: the inviting row of windows across the front of the building is gone, a victim of outward expan-sion.

MAYFLOWER DINER, 473 SOUTHERN ARTERY, ROUTE 3, QUINCY, MASSACHUSETTS   C-345

Postcard view of Mayflower #2, 1951. At that time there were, per Tom Galvin, seven diners in operation in Quincy. Now there's one. In North Quincy. And it's no prize.

MAYFLOWER DINER
QUINCY

Charlotte DiTullio, 52, fairly beamed when I mentioned the Mayflower. "We used to go there after church in the 1960s. My husband, his mother, and his aunt," she told me. "I was from the south (Tennessee), so diners were unique. I loved it! All the stainless steel. And you could see all the activity – the food preparation – going on. We'd have the big breakfast: eggs, toast, bacon, home fries. No oatmeal. Save that for the weekdays." Added Charlotte: "It was a fun, happy memory." I could tell.

The Mayflower was born in 1940. Its proprietor was Pete Calimeris. Its location was on the Southern Artery, #473, back when the Artery was Route 3: "the main road between Boston and Nantasket and all points south to Cape Cod,"

as phrased by Quincy historian Tom Galvin. Courtesy of Tom we are also treated (please see page 88) to a look at the initial Mayflower. It was one of but two double-ended streamliners manufactured by the Worcester Lunch Car Company, of Worcester, in response to the similar-looking Sterling Streamliners put out by rival J.B. Judkins Company, of Merrimac, Massachusetts.

As lovely as it was to look at, however, Pete's first Mayflower was small. The result: in 1950 he traded it in for a bigger model, located on the same site. This is the Mayflower pictured on this page, and that Charlotte and most people recall. Sam Kotoulas, who worked at the second Mayflower in the 1960s, … (cont'd. on page 88)

PETE & MURIEL'S
SOUTH MIDDLEBORO

Pete & Muriel's, located on the Cranberry Highway/Route 28, looks as if it should have featured carhops. Maybe even on roller skates. But it didn't. It was a sit-down or take-out affair that specialized in spaghetti & meatballs, charcoal broiled dishes, steak dinners, pizza, and ice cream.

Pete and Muriel Cammarata opened in 1956, converting what had been a house, built in 1930, into a restaurant. She is remembered as a big woman; he as being shorter than she. They are both remembered for their "locally famous" fried clams.

Pete and Muriel sold their place in 1976. There followed a string of other proprietors who gave the structure other names: Esterbrook's, The Cranberry Highway, Charlie's, more. Today the hip-roofed building is still, at least partially, an eating place. It is Capeway Convenience, selling pizza, grinders, and breakfast sandwiches as well as groceries, beer, wine, and assorted sundries. Employee Sandra Lawrence proudly pointed out that the Capeway's curved nine-stool counter is "original" Pete & Muriel's, as is the classic green Hamilton-Beech frappe maker. Sandra is especially proud of the latter.

Postcard view, circa 1962. There's a sizable addition on the back, but other than that not much has changed since this photo was taken. Even the sign is still intact, although the words have been changed. Well worthy of note: Sisson's, converted from a Middleboro, Wareham & Buzzards Bay Street Railway car into a diner in the late 1920s, is but a 1/4 mile up the road from the Capeway.

BOB'S CHARCOAL HOT DOGS
WILTON

"On Sunday nights you couldn't get near the place." Julia (Carvutto) Monroe, now 81, clearly enjoys talking about the "good old days" in the 1940s and 1950s when Bob's was a western Connecticut hamburger and hot dog hot spot. "People would come from all around…Norwalk, Stamford, Westport, Danbury, New Canaan, even New

and that they'd have 4-5 employees on both the day and the night shifts six days a week and then jump to 12-15 on Sundays. The hot dogs and hamburgers were the big draw, of course, but Bob's sold lots of milkshakes, soft drinks and coffee, and ice cream cones and sundaes, too. Everything came served on a tray which you'd bring back to your car.

BOB'S CHARCOAL HOT DOGS
JUNCTION ROUTE 7 and 33
WILTON, CONN.

ICE CREAM

BOB'S CHARCOAL HOT DOGS

Postcard view, circa 1950. Bob's was western Connecticut's 1950s' charcoal king.

York." They'd come because, per Julia, "There was nothing like the (taste of) charbroiled hamburgers and hot dogs."

Julia, who was the sister of proprietor Bob Carvutto and who worked at Bob's from its inception in 1946 until its demise in 1960, recalls that Bob's was "quite a big place,"

Bob's eventually closed, in October 1960, because, smiles Julia, "I got married and he (brother Bob) had no one to run the operation at night." Bob's old building is still very much alive, however, as the Wilton Farm and Deli. Takeout is still big business. Trays are not.

PURITAN MAID
EAST HARTFORD

During its heyday before World War II there were at least six Puritan Maids serving central Connecticut. Begun in 1936-1937 by two brothers who'd made it big in the trucking business, Clarence and Harry Woolridge, there were units in Avon, Farmington, Hartford, East Hartford, Windsor, elsewhere. The leader of the pack was the Puritan Maid featured here, the one at 476 Connecticut Boulevard in East Hartford. It was a structure with a split personality. To adults it was a good place to grab a meal; to the area's teenagers it was *the* place to hang out. "It had a jukebox," beams Doris Suessman (who's 81 now but was a teenager then) "and it was glorious because we could buy an ice cream soda or a sandwich and listen to the jukebox. It was like going out rather than going to someone's house."

Things changed when the war came along. With gas rationing in effect there were less motorists. To compensate, Clarence and Harry added liquor to the menu. That lead to the end of the teenage trade. The East Hartford Puritan Maid served its last meal in 1946. It was then converted into Goldie Motors, a Studebaker showroom. As such it lasted until 1950. Next came a used car dealership. Then, in the early 1960s, demolition. The site is now occupied by Newman Chevrolet.

Postcard view, circa 1940

Puritan Maid RESTAURANT
CONNECTICUT BLVD. -- EAST HARTFORD, CONN.

Matchbook cover, circa 1940. "Everything was cooked right there in front of you," remembers 84-year old Dan Buell. Dan liked that.

SHORE LINE DINER
CLINTON

Frank Verry must have liked Clinton: he had a hand in bringing not one, but two, diners to town. He and partner Crist Ferraro had number one on the way in circa 1931...and on the way out circa 1932 (please see page 35). Shortly thereafter Frank brought another diner to Clinton, set it up in a different location, and named it the Shore Line. His involvement with this second Clinton diner, though, was shortlived. He had a problem finding adequate help to staff both eateries. The result: Frank decided to focus on his Westbrook operation (again, please see page 35). He sold the Shore Line to the first in a succession of owners who kept the diner going through the late 1950s. Clinton native Dan Buell, 84, well recalls the Shore Line as "a gathering place." He especially remembers the diner's pot roast and hamburg steak as worthy of note. Eighty-five year old Anthony "Tony" Bloom has his memories, too. "We used to go there (the Shore Line) all the time, the whole gang, after dances at the Grove Beach Casino." This was in the early thirties. "Before I got married," reminisces Tony, with a pronounced twinkle in his eye. "It was a great place. They had great hamburgers and onions."

The memories became history when the Shore Line closed and was demolished, circa 1960. Part of the diner lives on, though. "When they started taking all the equipment out," recalls Stuart Colby, 72, "the Congregational Church got the grill." And Stuart's quite confident it's still there. The Shore Line's old site, at 86 East Main (Boston Post Road/ U.S. Route 1), is now occupied by a newish building that houses Saldamarco's Italian Deli.

Fiske House menu design, August 22, 1915. "This hotel in itself is one of the many elements that has given Damariscotta the prestige it enjoys as a summer resort and rendezvous for automobile parties." Booklet, HISTORIC DAMARISCOTTA, 1910.

THE FISKE HOUSE
DAMARISCOTTA

The Fiske House, opened as a three-story hotel / eatery by D. (Decator) E. Fiske in 1904, was noted for excellent cuisine, fine service, and satisfied clientele that included "automobilists" and local folks alike. Plus menus, daily menus at that, that were a visual delight.

In spite of all of the above, however, the Fiske House fell upon hard times during the Depression, closing in the late 1930s. The structure then served as an American Legion post and recreation center for Damariscotta's youth. During World War II it housed Company C of the 181st Infantry, 26th Yankee Division.

The once-renowned inn was demolished in 1957 to make way for a bank. "It was," notes Richard B. Day, president of the Damariscotta Historical Society, "a sad day for historic preservationists!"

FISKE HOUSE

D. E. FISKE, PROPRIETOR
DAMARISCOTTA, MAINE
SUNDAY, AUGUST 22, 1915

THE CROSSROADS
OXFORD

The building that housed the Crossroads has lived three lives. Life number one, starting in 1935, was as a diner. Ken Devault, 70, vividly recalls those days: "I was a little fellow then. It (the diner) really turned me on. It looked like a train." Around 1940 a large addition, clearly visible on the left in the view featured here, was appended to the original diner in order to turn the Crossroads (so named for its location where Massachusetts' Route 56 crosses U.S. Route 20) into a more full-fledged restaurant and night spot. Lifelong resident Harry Jolly, 85, notes "That was before the Mass. Pike (had been constructed) and there was a lot of traffic on Route 20."

Under different proprietors and different names – The Embers, Kastle's Keep, Manhattan's – what was the Crossroads steadily evolved less and less into food service and more and more into show biz. When I visited in January 2000 the building, looking not the least like it does here, had recently been transformed into Centerfolds 2000, an "adult entertainment complex." I shared the postcard shown here with the manager. He was not visibly impressed.

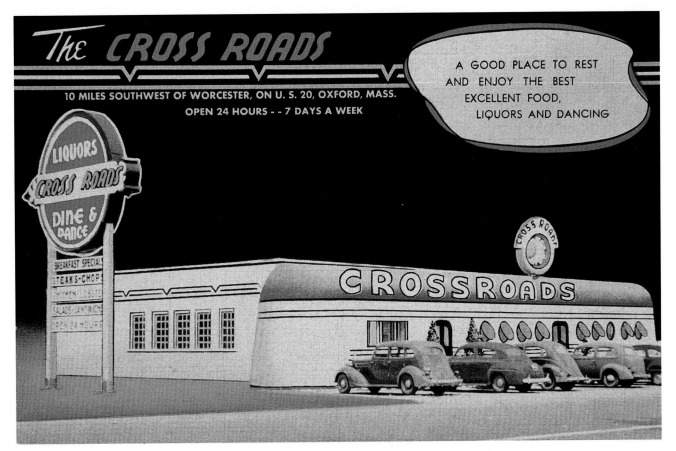

Postcard view, circa 1940. Stretching over 3,000 miles from Boston to Toledo, Oregon, U.S. Route 20 has seen many, many eating places. The Crossroads was one of them.

Matchbook cover, circa 1940

MARKET SQUARE DINER
CHICOPEE

When I asked former Market Square Diner proprietor Bob Theroux what his hours had been he laughed and replied "How many hours are there?" It turns out that the old "threw the keys away" story was true for Bob's father, Bill "Winkie" Theroux. When Bill opened in 1928 he really opened: the Market Square operated 24 hours a day 365 days of the year. Winkie felt that "There's always some people out there that have to eat."

The Market Square, located at 253 Front Street, was constructed by the Wason Manufacturing Company, a dining car builder located in nearby Springfield. When Winkie went to the bank to borrow money to pay for the diner, the banker, laughs Bob, wanted to know what his father had in the way of collateral. Winkie's reply: "I have eight kids." He got the loan.

Bob, who worked in the diner almost from infancy, recalls that his father put out a soup-to-pie complete dinner for 45¢ in the early thirties. He also recalls that Winkie often gave away more food than he sold during those Depression times. There was always free beef stew, apple pie, and coffee for anyone who needed it.

Bob and his dad (mostly Bob, he admits) remodeled the diner and added an annex, too, in 1966. As a result a name change seemed in order. Bob chose "Embassy Grill." "It's a classy name," he laughs as he says it.

Bill "Winkie" Theroux died in 1967. Bob then ran the diner alone until 1978 when the City of Chicopee decided to enlarge the square for which the diner had been named. Rather than relocate, Bob sold the diner to a man who moved it to South Hadley for use as part of a night club complex. It has seemingly been embroiled in zoning issues ever since. The result is that the Market Square/Embassy sits unoccupied and unused. Not lost… but certainly not exactly in full bloom, either.

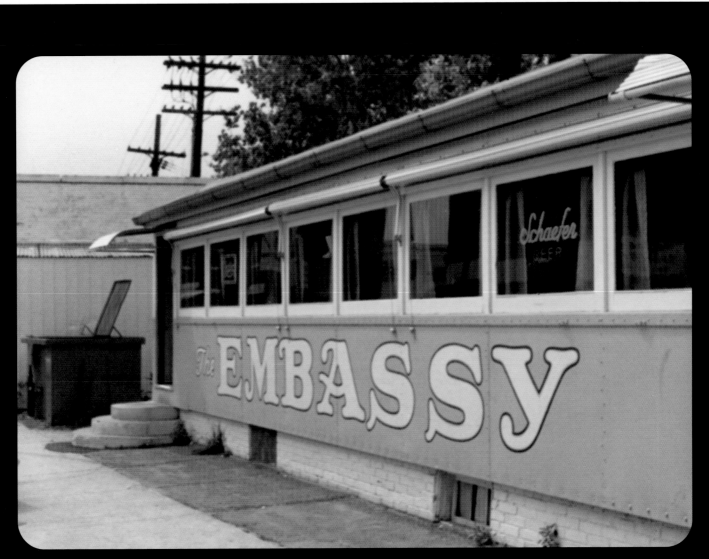

Photo, circa 1970. Courtesy of Bob Theroux, Chicopee.
Bob thought that "Embassy" was a "classy name."

MAYFLOWER DINER
QUINCY (cont'd. from page 79)

…remembers it as "a beautiful diner, inside and outside." Carol Damiano, 50, recalls that the booths were comfortable; the atmosphere and the service friendly. Barbara Neil, Quincy High class of 1949, recalls that after bowling, or a ballgame or most anything you'd go to the Mayflower "for coffee, an English muffin, and a chat." Barbara still recalls the name of her favorite Mayflower waitress, too. It was Gertrude: "She was a nice person."

Pete Calimeris sold the Mayflower in 1966. It closed more than a decade later, in 1977 or 1978, and was demolished. On its old site there is now a McDonald's.

MAYFLOWER DINER - ON ROUTE 3, 473 SOUTHERN ARTERY, QUINCY, MASSACHUSETTS

Postcard view of Mayflower #1, probably 1940/1941. Courtesy of Tom Galvin, Quincy. This rare postcard depicts an equally rare diner. The Mayflower was a Worcester Lunch Car Company double-ended streamliner…one of only two ever produced.

SEVIGNY'S (7E'S)
QUINCY

Charles P. Sevigny began making and selling candy out of the Sevigny family home at 7 Bass Street in Quincy in 1926. The family moved to the "big time," a stand on the Southern Artery/Route 3 (now 3A), in 1933. Clams and other seafood goodies were successfully added in 1938. "When you wanted fried clams or seafood you'd go to Sevigny's (later simplified to 7E's)," recalls Quincy native Barbara Neil, 68. "My husband and I used to take our kids there," beamed Margaret Fasano, 63. "We'd say 'Who wants to go to Sevigny's?' and they'd get all excited. They loved the clams!" Others recall Sevigny's ribbon candy. "It was the thinnest candy you could get," is what John Noonan, 80, remembers, while for 62-year old Audrey Wilcoxen it was the brightly colored Christmas variety she liked the best.

The Sevigny family bowed out of the business that bore their name in the late 1950s, but a succession of other operators kept customers happy until 1968. Today the Sevigny's old location, at 527 Southern Artery, is occupied by a Dunkin' Donuts' parking lot.

Postcard view, circa 1945. Courtesy of Tom Hug, Vermilion, Ohio. "When you wanted fried clams or seafood you'd go to Sevigny's."

SELECT YOUR OWN LOBSTER FROM OUR POUND

Postcard view, circa 1950. Courtesy of Tom Hug, Vermilion, Ohio. On this site now, just over the Wareham line from Bourne, there is a rather scruffy-looking gas station and repair shop.

BUTTERMILK BAY, BUZZARDS BAY, MASS.   49949

SILVER MOON SEA GRILL
BUTTERMILK BAY, WAREHAM

The Silver Moon began operation in 1935. Its owners were Sam, Beis, and Mike Akeke, three brothers who ran the Onset Cash Market and who were noted for their fine food and produce. "They knew their food and it was quality:" that's how 79-year old Betty Ames recalls the Akekes and the Silver Moon. She recalls it as "classy," too, with white linen tablecloths and white linen napkins, all "kept very nice." Seventy-two year old Francis Walsh concurs: "It was quite the place. They had outside lighting and nice landscaping and everything." Betty and Francis agree, also, that the Sea Grill's water view was "*very* pretty."

The Silver Moon Sea Grill served fresh seafood and a water view until 1959. The building was then, rather miraculously, jacked up and moved 1.2 miles further west on the Cranberry Highway, U.S. Route 6. Since then it's seen service as a Commonwealth of Massachusetts' Department of Education district office, a used truck sales and service headquarters, and a video store. It is now, bricked over and minus its distinctive roofline, home to a golfing equipment and apparel shop called Golf, Inc.

90

GILSON'S INN
MERRIMACK

Gilson's had roots in Hilleah Park, a popular summer retreat of the early 1900s. There were cottages, dances, a bathing beach, and a refreshment stand. Through the years that stand was added onto until it became the full-fledged structure you see here. Fay and Glenna Read, 89 and 82, recall it well. "I used to ride a bicycle down there to eat," laughs Glenna. "A hot dog would be a big treat." At one point there were outdoor movies. "Everybody," recollects Fay, "sat in their cars or stood around watching the movie." And dancing. It's what the couple remember most. There were booths along the sides and you'd dance in the middle. "To a jukebox," Glenna makes clear.

Glenna and Fay also make clear that changes in ownership came along about as often as selection changes in the jukebox. Gilson's, the crowning glory of Ralph Gilson, was just one more name change. That's too bad, because Ralph had worked his way from cook at Guilmette's Diner in Nashua to manager of the Kernwood Hotel, also in Nashua, to proprietor of his very own place. It was not to be his long, however: it opened in 1948 and closed, when he died, in 1953.

What had been Gilson's later became Sheila's Grove. That, too, ceased to exist when it was sold to developers in 1985. They leveled the place, constructing what is there now, a condominium named Horseshoe Pond.

Gilson's Inn — Dining Room and Coffee Shoppe

Postcard view, circa 1950. Where this storied restaurant once stood, on the Daniel Webster Highway/Route 3 six miles north of the Nashua city line, there is today a condominium complex.

ONE OF OUR ICE CREAM STANDS ON ROUTE 101, Milford, New Hampshire

Postcard view, circa 1950. There's a good news footnote to the Hayward Farms story. As LOST DINERS was going to press it was learned that one of Stanley Hayward's great nephews is planning to open an ice cream stand near where the original stood sometime in 2001. And, as phrased by Milford historian Bettina R. Mace, "The natives are excited!"

HAYWARD FARMS ICE CREAM STAND MILFORD

"Hayward Farms" and "ice cream" were almost synonymous in south central New Hampshire for the better part of five decades. The Milford stand you see here was built in 1939 by Stanley and Mimi Hayward. Hayward Farms had been in business as a dairy since 1905. It took Stanley and Mimi to get the firm into the production of ice cream.

Art Hayward, Stanley and Mimi's son, fondly recalls those ice cream years. His favorite creation was what Hayward Farms named – and trademarked – a Walk Away Sundae: vanilla ice cream, real strawberries, and real whipped cream. Hot fudge, hot butterscotch, and banana splits followed in favor. Then there was ginger ice cream, too. "It," notes Art, "was one of our popular flavors." Sad to say, as he points out, no one even makes it anymore.

Hayward Farms eventually operated a string of six dairy stands across southern New Hampshire before hard times set in. As told by Art: "From the late '50s till the early '80s selling a quality ice cream was very difficult. People thought the size of their serving made it good." By the mid-1980s the value of the land on which the Milford stand was located had increased to the point where the seasonal retailing of ice cream and sandwiches was secondary. The stand was demolished. On the site, on Route 101 one and a half miles outside of town, there is now an Agway distribution center.

Matchbook covers, top, circa 1935; bottom, circa 1945. Courtesy of Frank Mooney, Nashua. Both Yankee Flyers were "Yankee" in construction as well as in name. Yankee Flyer I was a "Worcester," manufactured by the Worcester Lunch Car Company of Worcester, Massachusetts. Yankee Flyer II was a "Sterling Streamliner," manufactured by the J.B. Judkins Company of Merrimac, Massachusetts.

YANKEE FLYER
NASHUA

Legend has it that in 1925 a pair of entrepreneurial friends from Haverhill, Massachusetts stopped to visit an old associate in Nashua while enroute to Keene to look at a possible restaurant site. The pair, Bill Reich and Chris Kyriax, knew almost nothing about running a restaurant. They only knew they wanted to give it a try. During their Nashua sojourn the partners, as these things happen, came upon the Main Street Diner, located downtown at 221 Main. Before the day was through, legend has it again, they'd purchased said diner.

The new restaurateurs ran the Main Street as a solo operation until 1930 when they added a second diner, which they named the Yankee Flyer, to their "empire." An opening day ad in the April 16th *Nashua Telegraph* promised "The last word in Dining Cars, equipped to give the public of Nashua the best of food and service," and touted broiled steak, chops, chicken and lobster. Subsequent ads talked up the new diner's "Delicious Salads and Other Dainties" as well as an extensive lineup of homemade pies.

(cont'd. on page 127)

BOB'S DINER
BAINBRIDGE

You'd never guess that Betty Armstrong is 90 years old. And sitting with her on the back porch of her home in July 2000, she certainly wasn't. She was 25. And the year was 1935, the year she and her husband, Robert Francis ("Bob") Armstrong, opened Bob's Diner on bustling Route 7, the main street of Bainbridge. "We opened December 5th," Betty reminisces. "We hadn't intended to open until a few days later, but people saw the lights on at night and they came in. There was nothing like that (a diner) around there."

When I showed Betty a copy of the matchbook cover pictured here she beamed. "Everything (it says) there is true," she said. "We did everything ourselves. We had a farm and used a lot (of provisions) from there." Then there were the pies. Pie-making – at first handled by Bob's mom, Blanche; later by Betty – was serious business at Bob's.

Betty cherishes all the wonderful people who came to the diner through the years. Glenn Miller and his orchestra stopped in. So did the wrestler, Gorgeous George. "He had his hair up in curlers," Betty half chuckles and half blushes.

Bob passed away in 1984. Betty kept the diner going until 1990. "Then I couldn't handle it anymore," she states. After being closed for several years the diner was purchased by local businessman John W. Payne. Payne's announced intention was to restore the diner. Instead he ended up, in June 1994, tearing it down. (Not the normally prescribed way to restore something.). On the site today, opened in December 1994, is a new Bob's Diner. It would win few beauty contests.

Matchbook cover, circa 1940. Bob's was built on site. It had, nevertheless, that "real" diner appearance. "It looked like a caboose," Betty recalls with an obvious fondness. When the diner was demolished in 1994 "I felt," she says, "like somebody hit me in the stomach."

KENDALL TOURIST CAMP — 1½ MILES WEST OF SILVER CREEK, N. Y.

MOTOR ROUTE U. S. 20 — PHONE SILVER CREEK 40-J   4A-H572

Postcard view, circa 1940. Courtesy of Tom Hug, Vermilion, Ohio

Seventy-two year old Tom Roberts ate at the Kendall as a kid. He recalls it as a "good-sized diner," and that "they had it looking real nice." Village of Silver Creek Historian Agnes "Pat" Pfleuger reports that hamburgers, homemade pies, and Italian dishes were the sales mainstays.

KENDALL DINER
SILVER CREEK

Silver Creek was at one time home to not only a diner but to a rather substantial diner manufacturing company as well. That company was Ward and Dickinson. Founded by Charles Ward and Lee F. Dickinson in 1923, it remained operative until just before World War II. Some of Ward and Dickinson's diners were shipped as far as Michigan (and eastern Massachusetts: see pages 70-71). Some remained closer to home. The Kendall remained the closest of all.

The Kendall was part of a tourist complex that also included 49 furnished cabins (one for each of the then 48 states plus the District of Columbia) and a service station. It was built, most likely in the early thirties, by the Kendall Motor Oil Company and operated by Silver Creek native Ray Damon.

The Kendall complex – diner, service station and all 49 cabins – appears to have come to the beginning of the end in June 1945. That's when Ray Damon decided he'd rather sell cars than hamburgers and he opened Damon Motors in downtown Silver Creek. The diner was subsequently demolished to make way for a reconstruction of U.S. Route 20.

You Can't Eat In It… But You Can Sure Admire It

In the early 1990s the good citizens of Silver Creek raised $10,000 to restore a Ward and Dickinson dining car that had been sitting and rotting on the outskirts of town. It today sits proudly in front of the Municipal Building on Central Avenue. And it's worth a visit.

Postcard view, circa 1950. Maria tells the story of the time a group of first-time hunters from New York City pulled into the diner with a dead bull tied to the top of their car. "It had horns," said one of the group.

PATRICK'S
DINER
Highland
New York

PATRICK'S DINER
HIGHLAND

Patrick's story goes back to 1898, when Anthony Patrick came to America from Greece. He eventually went back to Greece, but left a bank account for his son, also Anthony ("Tony"), to open a business in America. Tony did not disappoint. He came to America in 1932 and "cut his teeth" as proprietor of a couple of places in neighboring New Paltz. Patrick's came along in 1945-1946. It was a family affair: Tony and sons Charles, Clarence, and James. "It was James who pretty much ran it, though," his daughter Allison Alsdorf, 54, told me.

James had been trained to be a cook in World War II. It paid off. People in Highland still talk about the diner's food: pancakes (77-year old Rose Lowery remembers a "special batter"), meatloaf, and, of course, pies. "It (Patrick's) was known for a great piece of pie," states Allison.

With Tony getting on (he would die in 1962), the Patricks leased their diner to Poughkeepsie-native Maria Bliziotis in 1960. Maria likes to tell how couples would want a certain booth. "Their booth." That they'd get upset if someone else were sitting there. "They were so in love," she laughs, "you could've given them raw potatoes and they would've said 'Aren't these great.' As long as it was 'their booth.'"

Maria left when she and her husband, yet another Anthony, purchased the College Diner in New Paltz in 1964. In 1965 Patrick's took on a new name: the Highland Diner. A far worse fate befell it in 1990: it was dismantled and replaced by a new diner/restaurant, the Gateway. Yes, there are pieces of the old diner within the new, but Patrick's is mostly history. Gateway proprietor Frank Georgakopoulos still gets customers who "remember," though. Especially a woman who comes in and inevitably says "I recall when I was a waitress (at Patrick's) and I made $3.00 a day. With tips."

McCANN'S DINER
HIGHLAND

Highland, thanks to being on U.S. Route 9W, was once a two-diner town. McCann's, located on the Mid-Hudson Bridge traffic circle, was diner number two. It arrived just after Patrick's was set up, in early 1946. That didn't make Tony Patrick any too happy. McCann's remained in operation until circa 1964 when it was removed to make way for a new bridge approach.

RHINEBECK DINER
RHINEBECK

"World's largest, most modern diner." So it states on the address side of the postcard on view here, adding, "Built at a cost of $75,000. Seating capacity 136 with private dining room seating 64."

The diner you see here, the "World's Largest," opened in May 1938. There had been an earlier Rhinebeck Diner. However, with ten stools and four tables, it was, at best, "Rhinebeck's Largest." This original diner was purchased by Greek immigrants Tony and Mary Djinis in 1931. Under their direction business flourished and the couple purchased the big beauty (a "Silk City," manufactured by the Paterson Vehicle Co., of Paterson, N.J.) you're looking at.

The impending arrival of the diner caused quite a stir, with *The Rhinebeck Gazette* endeavoring to keep readers posted. "The kitchen section, measuring fourteen by thirty feet, arrived Thursday afternoon and was quickly placed in position over the foundation that had been prepared," ran the April 29th edition, continuing "The huge main section, fourteen feet wide and fifty-five feet long, was hauled as far as Staatsburg Thursday night." *The Gazette* further noted that "A special permit was required to haul it (the diner) over the road in this state and it could be moved only during the daylight hours."

A May 6th clipping described the diner as "stainless steel and tile throughout, with mahogany finish trim and a color scheme of cream and blue predominating." Continued *The Gazette*: "Mrs. Djinis personally selected the color scheme."

The Djinises owned and operated the Rhinebeck Diner until their retirement in 1959. Purchased by a Kingston businessman, the diner was put on wheels and towed across the Kingston-Rhinecliff Bridge to a new location on Albany Avenue in Kingston in 1964. There it served, in succession, as a diner, an electronics supply store, and a diner/nightclub. In 1998 the diner was moved across the Hudson again, to Wappingers Falls. There it sits in storage. For sale. Don't rush to Wappingers, however, unless you have a spare $450,000 or so: that's the asking price.

Ad, HUDSON VALLEY VOLUNTEER FIREMEN'S ASSOCIATION 50th ANNIVERSARY YEAR BOOK, 1939. For their Grand Opening Day of May 7, 1938, Tony and Mary had 500 carnations on hand to be given away to patrons. They ran out before day's end. (Note: "Djines" is misspelled in the ad. It should be "Djinis.")

Postcard view showing the Rhinebeck Diner
as it appeared circa 1940. It was large!

Photo. The Riverside number one as it appeared in October 1945. Courtesy of Library of Congress, Washington, D.C. "This diner depends on truckers for its trade," noted the photographer.

RIVERSIDE DINER
CORTLAND/HOMER

The name "Riverside" has had a rather engaging history in Cortland/Homer diner circles. Ditto the name "Midway." This is their story.

In 1939 the Riverside Diner opened at 144 South Main Street/U.S. Route 11 in Homer. In that same year, on June 2nd, the Midway (Its ads noted it was "Midway between Cortland-Homer") Diner opened at 197 Homer Avenue/U.S. Route 11, Cortland. This latter diner, the original Midway, opened and closed under different owners until 1948 when it was either moved or, more likely, demolished. The Riverside, meanwhile, hummed along. Eighty-year old Willis Streeter recalls hefty portions. Especially pancake portions: "They'd put out a stack about 5" or so high. There was a stack!" Audrey Walberger, 74, worked at the Riverside as a waitress in the early 1940s. She, too, recalls large portions. Her own favorite was raspberry pie topped with a plentiful supply of chocolate ice cream. An amazing thing about the Riverside, *this* Riverside, was the sheer number of individuals who took a turn at owning/ operating it. By my count there were ten through the years.

Those years ended in 1964, when the diner and its surrounding area were leveled to make way for Interstate 81.

Two diners down. Let's back up to 1953, though. In that year a diner was moved from elsewhere (most people say Ithaca) and set up on North Homer Avenue/U.S. Route 11 on the Cortland/Homer border. It was named the Midway. Not in honor of the earlier Midway but because it, too, was halfway between downtown Cortland and downtown Homer. Midway II, if you will, was moved about a number of times before it finally settled just over the Homer side of the boundary line. It also changed names a number of times. In the late 1970s it was Drake's Diner; in the early eighties, Tommy's Restaurant.

Enter Garry Slack. A longtime food service man, Garry purchased the diner in 1982. At first, he laughs, he was going to rename it "The" (as in "Let's go to *The*"), but was – mercifully – talked out of it. You can probably guess, though, what Garry *did* name his diner. "I had a partner, Malcolm Sykes, who owned the Riverside Motel (just

Photo, circa 1960. Courtesy of Garry Slack, Cortland. Midway Diner #2 as it looked prior to becoming Riverside #2.

across Route 11) and we decided to tie the two (businesses) together," he explains. So "Riverside"/"Garry's Riverside" it became (with neither partner having any knowledge of the first Riverside's existence).

Garry, with appreciable help from his wife Sue and other family members, ran the diner until 1990. He's proudest of his French onion soup, his gravies,

his homebaked pies. The end for Garry's Riverside came early in the morning of January 20, 1990. The diner, in spite of the best efforts of 40 Homer firefighters, burned to the ground. Its former site, immediately to the left of Natoli's Route 11 Grocery, is now an open field/parking lot.

Photo, circa 1985. Courtesy of Garry Slack, Cortland. Riverside #2 – Garry's Riverside – about five years before its unfortunate demise.

Matchbook cover, circa 1935. "Kooler Keg Beer" and "Finest Food At Popular Prices": Spall's, as notes Rochester-area history buff Jim Starkman, had it all.

SPALL'S HOTEL
SEA BREEZE
(IRONDEQUOIT)

Located on a slice of land between Lake Ontario and Irondequoit Bay, the Sea Breeze area of Irondequoit has long been home to an array of eateries. Some, per local historian Patricia Wayne, have even offered "fine dining." Whether Spall's, owned and operated by George Spall from 1934 until circa 1940, was in that category is questionable. It would be difficult, however, to find displeasure with George's prices. The hotel's former site is now a vacant lot.

TED'S DINER
UTICA

Ted's opened in 1940, occupying the former Jack & Andy's Diner begun in 1932 by brothers Jack and Andy Gunn. Ted's was the creation of Theodore Camesano, an Italian native who came to America and Utica at age 20 in 1900. After working most of his life for the New York Central Railroad, Camesano moved into the diner business as manager of the National Diner, located at 828 Noyes Street in Utica. That was 1934, six years before making the big move to owning and operating his own place.

Theodore Camesano ran Ted's until 1944 when he retired, turning the diner over to his son, also named Theodore. Theodore the younger carried on in his dad's footsteps until 1960, closing the diner just about the same time Theodore, Sr. died, in July. On the diner's old site, 136 North Genesee Street, there is now a Hess Gas Station.

Postcard view, circa 1954. I ran into lifelong Utica resident Jim Testa sitting on a bench near where Ted's used to be. He told me that Elvis stopped at Ted's for a meal while on tour in the 1950s. I asked him why "The King" ate at Ted's. "Because he was hungry," answered Jim. It was a good answer.

"There's Nothing Finer Than Ted's Diner"
134 N. Genesee St., Utica, N. Y. 2-9375

TEXACO GRILLE
GENEVA

For the story of the Texaco Grille please turn to pages 148-149.

Postcard view, 1949. During World War II, business – especially from close-by Sampson Navy Training Center – was so brisk that fences had to be put up to keep the hungry hoards in line.

VINCIGUERRA'S BELLEVUE DINER SCHENECTADY

Pretty girls have long been utilized to adorn advertising. Especially advertising aimed at males. Beer. Bars. Sometimes diners...as with James "Jimmy" Vinciguerra and his Bellevue Diner.

The Bellevue – named after the section of town in which it stood rather than any scenic Schenectady splendor it over-looked – came to be in 1956, when Vinciguerra took over what had been Frank's Salon and transformed it into a diner-shaped restaurant. It was a venture that should have been right up Jimmy's alley: he'd been a restaurant cook and/or proprietor at various places in Schenectady since at least 1946. Alas, though, Vinciguerra's stay with the Bellevue was to be shortlived. By late 1958 he'd moved on to being proprietor of the local Town Tavern. His former diner, its name shortened to just "Bellevue," remained up and running until 1962. Yellow Page ads for the early 1960s tout home-made doughnuts, jumbo queen steak sandwiches, hot and cold dinners.

The Bellevue's old address, most recently home to the King and Queen's Unisex Salon ("Hair design by Michele"), is now deserted and sadly forlorn. It clearly looks, however, like a restaurant should...and perhaps somewhere inside the "All American Girl" is getting ready to serve up a Queen Steak Sandwich.

ALL AMERICAN GIRL

VINCIGUERRA'S BELLEVUE DINER
2147 Broadway ·:· Phone FR. 2-9792
SCHENECTADY, NEW YORK
Famous For Queen Steak Sandwiches

January 1958

SUN	MON	TUE	WED	THU	FRI	SAT
			1	2	3	4
5	6	7	8	9	10	11
12	13	14	15	16	17	18
19	20	21	22	23	24	25
26	27	28	29	30	31	

Calendar, 1958. The artwork you see here was stock calendar art. Jimmy Vinciguerra had hundreds of images – including many another attractive female face – from which to choose. He selected the "All American Girl." It was an excellent choice.

WALDORF RESTAURANT & GRILL
JOHNSON CITY

It was difficult to miss the Waldorf Restaurant & Grill sign in downtown Johnson City. It was big. Twelve feet tall, at least, according to long-time owner Charles "Chuck" Ciufo.

The Waldorf was begun by Nick Alskaris around the time Prohibition ended, around 1933. Chuck's father, Mike Ciufo, bought it in 1938. Always as much a bar as a grill, the Waldorf was nonetheless quite an eating place. "On Sunday we used to have a $1.00 smorgasbord," remembers Chuck. "All kinds of salads and meat dishes. People would really turn out for that." Then there was halorki, an eastern European dish made with rice, hamburger, and cabbage.

Wednesday was dime sandwich night. Good customers for all of the happenings included the Binghamton Triplets (Eastern League) baseball team. "They'd come in after games," Chuck fondly recalls. "It was a jumpin' joint back then" (in the 1940s and 1950s), interjects Chuck's wife Catherine.

The "jumpin' " came to an end in 1994. That's when Chuck decided it was time to retire. The Restaurant & Grill's old stand, at 235 Main Street, is today occupied by an Asian grocery.

Main Street Looking West, Johnson City, N. Y.

9A-H2289

Postcard view, 1939. The Waldorf and its marvelous neon sign are on the right. The sign was taken down circa 1985. "The town was afraid it would fall down," remembers Helen Aton, who worked at the Waldorf at the time. "But," she laughs, "the guy who took it down said the building would have fallen down before the sign."

WOODWORTH'S RESTAURANT
GENEVA

If buildings could talk this is one that might well find itself with a large and appreciative audience. It's had a history. A Cornell University Preservation Planning study in 1979 dates the front of the building to at least 1870. At first utilized as a grocery store, the structure became a private residence circa 1885. Next, soon after the turn of the century, came a saloon. During its saloon days the building was slated to be demolished to make way for a church that was to be moved to the site. The church, however, burned to the ground while still resting on its rollers.

From 1920 on, the structure, located at 164 Castle Street, has been a restaurant of one sort or another. There was Bertram's, followed by Bertram & Guinan's, followed by Guinan's ("A Good Place to Eat"). In 1937 the structure became the Castle Diner (aka Fairchild's Restaurant). In 1947 Don L. Woodworth (see also pages 148-149) took control. The result: Castle Diner became Woodworth's Restaurant. Don hedged his bets, though, by continuing to use the Castle Diner name, too.

Don Woodworth ran Woodworth's through 1957. Since then the building has been home to several eateries. It is now Wing Tai, an Asian restaurant.

Postcard view, 1949. This is actually a split image postcard. Half of it shows the Woodworth. Half of it shows the equally colorful Texaco Grille (see page 103). Don Woodworth owned them both.

CHAMPLAIN PARK
SHELBURNE

Nowadays the eating and lodging choices that line U.S. Route 7 south of Burlington almost overrun each other. Not so when Champlain Park came into being in 1932-1933. "It was pretty far from civilization," laughs 68-year old area-native Sonny Audette.

Champlain Park's first owners were Michael and Rose Schildhaus. They set the standard for what was to come: pump a little gas; sell a little food; rent a lot of cabins. The restaurant side of the operation was certainly secondary to the cabins. "I don't recall anything fancy coming out of there (the restaurant)," confided Shelburne Town Clerk Colleen Haag.

Champlain Park maintained its name and identity until purchased by a man named Howard Cranwell in 1957. Cranwell changed names to the Champlain Motor Court; replaced, over time, the cabins with attached motel units; and converted the restaurant building into a "modern" motel office. To accomplish this latter feat, Cranwell took the structure you see here and "gutted it" (per Colleen Haag) and/or "contemporized it" (per long-time area businessman Jack DuBrul, 66). Whatever, "Something happened to it." (per long-time area restaurateur Charlie Bissonette, 62).

The structure on view here yet exists in its "contemporized" form as the office for Shelburne Econo Lodge, the entity that replaced the Champlain Motor Lodge in 1990. When I showed the postcard pictured here to the Econo Lodge clerk on duty the day I was there and told her that this was how her building used to look, she said "It's hard to believe." And I said, "I agree."

Postcard view, circa 1940. If you'd like to admire a more-fully-surviving old-time Shelburne eatery, drive on down Route 7 a little over a mile from Econo Lodge, located at 1961 Shelburne Road, until you come upon the Dutch Mill, located at 4385 Shelburne Road. Born the Windmill in 1927, the Dutch Mill is today the pride and joy of Jamie Bissonette and family. Do not miss the old photo collection just inside the 63-year old eatery's front door.

Matchbook cover, circa 1940. Courtesy of the American Diner Museum, Providence. Where Burns Pullman Diner used to brighten the day with its "Roasted, Toasted, Frankforts" there is now an empty lot.

BURNS PULLMAN DINER
PROVIDENCE

It should've been Mrs. Burns all spiffed up and on display here. That's because it was Mrs. Burns – Viola L. – who started Burns Pullman in 1929, not her hubby, Harry. Sure, Harry was probably there, but city directories of the day do not show him as officially involved until 1938. The couple lived in nearby Cranston, and commuted to Providence to run their venture. Until 1947, that is, when a man named Samuel Lozow took over, beginning a succession of new owners and new names (Pullman Pancake House; Leon's Three G's; Kathleen's; the Phoenix) that continued until 1983 when the structure was demolished. There are those few in the neighborhood, though, who yet recall the diner's heyday. Dennis Driscoll, 63, remembers Burns as "quite a place: one of the big diners in Rhode Island in the 1950s."

Dennis' favorite was the diner's "Famous Roasted, Toasted, Frankforts." "They *were* good," he beams as he thinks back to those days many, many meals ago.

Pete and Oppie Bedrosian, both 73, have fond memories, too. "It (the food and service) was always good," stated Pete as he did his best to describe the diner's layout of a counter in front and booths in back. For Pete the counter was for hanging out with "the guys;" the booths for hanging out with Oppie. "We wouldn't have anything fancy," smiles Oppie. "A BLT or a meatball sandwich." Whatever, it paid off. The couple has been married 50 years. Burns Pullman Diner may be history, but Pete and Oppie are still hanging out.

PETE'S LUNCH
SPRINGFIELD

"Sure I remember Pete's," Holyoke native Neil Sutter told me after I'd stopped him as he was walking along Dwight Street in downtown Springfield. "I used to work for the old New England Telephone Company (Neil points to a huge brick building), park for $4.00 a month (he stresses "a month" and points again), and eat lunch there (one final point). Unfortunately, "there" is now a parking lot. But to Neil it's a place where he and his fellow workers enjoyed many a meal. "They put out a nice lunch," he recalls. "Good sandwiches. Hamburg specials. Soups."

Pete's lunch opened in 1932 with Peter Valaoris (often misspelled "Valsoras") and Theodore Sotirios as proprietors. In 1937 Satirios moved back to his native Greece. Pete, however, stayed on. In fact, in 1938 he expanded his "empire" by taking on management of the Station View Grill, located around the corner at 70 Liberty Street. Both eateries were open 24 hours a day and promised the time-honored duo of "Good Food" and "Reasonable Prices."

In 1951 Pete divested himself of the Station View. A year later, in 1952, he did the same with his namesake lunch. Pete bounced back briefly as owner/operator of Pete's Diner in West Springfield in 1953. In 1954 he and his wife Mary moved to New Brunswick, New Jersey. As for Pete's Lunch, it remained in operation, under a succession of owners, through 1955.

Match book cover, circa 1945

Photo, circa 1952. Courtesy of Holyoke
History Room, Holyoke Public Library.

PURITAN DINER
HOLYOKE

It's amazing what people will remember. Four and a half decades after the fact what does lifelong Holyoke resident Johnny Leja, now 57, recall about the Puritan Diner? Not the food. He never ate there. Not the counter or the booths. He never set foot inside the door. No, Johnny recalls the Puritan's ads in Holyoke's then daily newspaper, *The Holyoke Transcript*. "They were always advertising for dishwashers," he laughs. "I was just a kid, but I saw those ads and I wanted the job. When you're twelve," he says with a certain panache, "and you're a paperboy, being a dishwasher is moving on up. A career year." (Johnny, incidentally, is a distant cousin to Holyoke's own Frank Leja, a rather storied Yankee "Bonus Baby" of the mid-1950s.).

The Puritan Diner began operations in 1930. Located at 1608 Northampton Street/U.S. Route 5, it was an offshoot of Puritan Oil, which ran a Sunoco station next door. Robert E. Young, a former employee at Deane Steam Pumps (known "affectionately" as Damned Small Pay by many who worked there), was the guiding light for both the gas station and the diner. New proprietors, in 1945, were Nat Hadez and Morris Zaidman. Others followed through 1962, when the diner was vacated and, it appears, torn down. Finding people who yet recall it, though, is not difficult. Don Breen, 73, best recalls the diner's giant rotary toaster. "That's the first thing you saw when you walked in. I had never seen one before. I thought it was a great idea." Don also recalls that the short order cook would "never turn around or take an order slip. He took it (the orders) all in verbally and," muses Don, "I guess he got it right all the time."

Harry Craven is about 20 years younger than Don. Harry is 55, and his memories revolve around the diner's chocolate milk. And its counter. "I was eight or nine and I'd go there all the time with my twin sister and our parents." Harry loved the chocolate milk. "It was probably the atmosphere, the ambiance," he admits. Harry also remembers the Puritan's booths and its counter. He much preferred the counter. "I got a bang out of sitting on the stool and the fact I could see all that was going on."

Ads for dishwashers; rotary toasters; amazing cooks; chocolate milk; counters and stools: the Puritan had something for everyone.

The Puritan Diner's former site is now occupied by the parking lot for a Bess Eaton Donuts.

RENO DINER
ORLEANS

The Reno Diner was the creation, in 1940, of one Joseph "Joe" Davis. Joe, according to his daughter Henrietta, was casting about for a new line of work. Operating a diner seemed a good choice. He had an orchard next to his house on old Route 6, and he tore down a few of the trees and he and a cousin and an uncle and a friend built the diner. Joe called it "Reno" because there was a store in Orleans that sold Norge appliances and they, the store, had an extra neon sign they said Joe could have. The only name Joe could come up with that used some or all of the five letters in "Norge" was "Reno." Then it turned out Joe didn't use the sign anyway.

The Reno was closed during World War II because, as Henrietta puts it so well, "No one was on the road, what with gas rationing." After the war was over, though, it was back on track for the diner. Henrietta and her husband, Gordon Harris, were the new owner/operators. Gordon did the cooking (Henrietta: "He knew how to cook!") and Henrietta the bookkeeping. "Saturday night was the biggest thing," she recalls well. "All the other restaurants in Orleans would close at 11:00 or 12:00 and everybody would come to the diner for coffee or a snack after the movies."

Gordon and Henrietta sold the diner business in 1957. "He (Gordon) had just had it," Henrietta also recalls well. "It was too time consuming and he was there from the crack of dawn to late in the evening."

The diner was operated by the Demetras family for a year or two after 1957. Then they tore it down and built the motel (Orleans Holiday) that's still there today.

Postcard view, circa 1950. Notice the folks, doing their very best to be a part of the photo, lined up just inside the door.

TOM BUSH, THE HOT DOG KING
HANOVER, MASSACHUSETTS

"Tom Bush was known far and wide for his hot dogs and steamed rolls," recalls 86-year old Ethel Henderson Briggs of North Hanover, continuing "When you had a date with a fellow, the place to go would be Tom Bush's for a hot dog." Ninety-four year old Leander Nichols of the Four Corners section of Hanover agrees: "People would go out after supper, just go for a spin, and stop at Tom Bush's and have a hot dog with mustard and relish. There were no tables nor stools…you just stood up there to the counter, ordered your hot dogs and took them back to your car to eat them."

Tom Bush was a one-man show (Ethel Henderson Briggs remembers he wore a white apron) who set up to sell his frankfurts (they were boiled and he sold them for 10¢ apiece) in the mid-1920s and closed down in the very early 1930s. Hanover Town Historian Barbara Barker suspects it was the coming of the Depression that did Tom Bush and his hot dogs in. I suspect she's right.

Tom Bush's former stand on Hanover Street is today incorporated into a building that houses Pooch Paws, a dog grooming business.

When Out Touring Be Sure And Pay A Visit To

Tom Bush

THE HOT DOG KING

West Hanover, Mass.   Tel. Rockland 8650-M

Frankfurts may come and frankfurts may go,

But patrons come for my hot dogs forever.

There's a Reason   Try One   They're Different

Ad, *The Hanoverian*, the magazine of Sylvester High School, Hanover, June 1928

WINDMILL INN
EAST CHARLEMONT

No book on northeast roadside travels would be complete without the Mohawk Trail, that historic and scenic route (Route 2 / 2A) that stretches across northwestern Massachusetts to the New York line. Plus I find the view of the Windmill Inn to be especially inviting. Almost certainly the oldest structure in LOST DINERS – Gloria Jean Purington of the Charlemont assessor's office lists its age as "200 years plus or minus." – it is remembered as a well-known eating place from the 1920s into the 1940s. Todd Gerry, who owned and lived in the property from 1974 to 1994, told me that when he'd hold a lawn sale people would stop and invariably say "Oh, I recall eating here." Steak and spaghetti plates were the Windmill's best-known dishes.

The old inn, which sits several miles from "downtown" Charlemont and 1/3 of a mile east of Indian Plaza ("Largest Indian Trading Post On The Mohawk Trail"), is today a private residence. It looks a lot like the view shown here, but it can fool you, too. That's because the third floor dormers are gone. So's the outbuilding to the left. Otherwise, though, it's 1935 and the steaks are on the broiler.

WINDMILL INN, ON THE MOHAWK TRAIL.

EAST CHARLEMONT, MASS.

Postcard view, circa 1935. Present-day occupant Joe Celli got quite excited when I showed him this shot. He kept saying "That's my house!"

NEW HAMPSHIRE

Area: 9,304 sq. miles.

Population: 1,235,786

Scale: 1 inch = approximately 23 miles

Bartlett •

Chocorua •

• Lebanon

Laconia •

Manchester •

Hampton Falls •

Merrimack •

Milford •

Nashua •

The Bartlett Hotel
Bartlett, N. H.

Postcard view, circa 1950. Where the Bartlett once stood, at the northeast corner of Route 302 and River Street in uptown / downtown Bartlett, there is now a vacant lot. In the rear of the lot is a large sign that reads "Hotel Bartlett Parking." It is playing to an empty audience.

BARTLETT HOTEL
BARTLETT

Motorists have been driving to and through the White Mountains for over a century. Beautiful views and mountain air have been the major draws. But good food hasn't been far behind. The Bartlett provided all three. Opened as the Howard on July 1, 1912, the hotel was always ready to serve "automobile parties." It was located on U.S. Route 302 – nicknamed the "Theodore Roosevelt Highway" – which was originally meant to flow cross-country from Portland, Maine to Portland, Oregon.

"The dining room was big, and quite formal," recalls 85-year old Gertrude Murray of Danvers, Massachusetts, who ate at the hotel many times with her family when she was a youngster in the early 1930s. Gertrude laughs as she admits that what she recalls most vividly are the hotel's plates. "They were heavy and had a green border around them. All these years later Gertrude also remembers the hotel's eggs: how "fluffy" they were when scrambled.

The Bartlett continued to serve patrons well into the 1980s. In fact, per Bartlett historian Aileen M. Carroll, it was enjoying a renaissance under new owners when it burned to the ground in March of 1989.

Photo, February 1947. Courtesy of Emile Pouliot, Manchester. There's no need for a "circa" here. Someone from long ago etched "Feb. 1947" right into the photo. The blizzard of '47 was one to remember...but it didn't slow Eddie's down by even a beat.

EDDIE'S LUNCH
MANCHESTER

Reasoning that people who like to eat in diners today probably liked to eat in diners in the past, too, I stationed myself by the entrance to the Red Arrow, Manchester's sole remaining diner. I was rewarded with Arthur Lessard, as pleasant an interviewee as one is apt to find. Just the mention of Eddie's Lunch brought a big smile to his face. "I used to stop there everyday. Between this one (the Red Arrow) and that one I had a lot of meals." Continued Arthur, faster than I could possibly write: "It was a beautiful diner. It was one of the larger diners in the area. They had a large – real large – variety of meals. Their pan fries on the grill" – big smile – "were excellent." Words like "immaculate," "homey," "very popular," etc., etc. kept coming as Arthur, who's 74 and a Manchester native, tried to recapture Eddie's for me. "It drew a lot of French (i.e., Franco-American) trade. People would speak French. There was the old saying," Arthur smiled big again, "that you had to get a pass if you got over the Notre Dame Bridge (to West Manchester, home to both Eddie's and most of Manchester's considerable French population) and were Irish or other than French."

Photo, 1926. Courtesy of Emile Pouliot, Manchester. Eddie, left, and his staff shortly after Eddie had purchased the 24-Hour Lunch. You'll notice the absence of any and all females: it would not be 'til World War II that women would find appreciable employ in the diner business. During the war, however, with *man*power away in the service, "Rosie" became a waitress as well as a riveter.

CATERER

Eat

...AT...

EDDIE'S LUNCH
35 AMORY STREET
MANCHESTER, N. H.

TEL. 5591

Business card, circa 1940. Courtesy of Emile Pouliot, Manchester. Eddie widened out into catering in 1939. It proved a huge success. Eddie Pouliot's son Emile recounts that Eddie's Lunch brightened weddings and banquets all over New Hampshire and into Massachusetts as well. Especially big was the annual Rochester (New Hampshire) Fair. There Eddie served 1500 people and had to bring waitresses in by the busload. Emile also recalls that his dad was often called upon to sing French songs, especially Alouette. Even at *Irish* weddings.

Edouard J. Pouliot was definitely French. And very proud of it. Born in Winthrop, Maine, he moved to Manchester as a teenager in 1910. After service in the Navy during World War I, he returned to the Queen City of the Merrimack and, in 1921, jumped into the city's lunch cart business with a cart stationed on South Main Street/Granite Square.

In 1926 Eddie branched out, purchasing the five-year old 24-Hour Lunch, located at 35 Amory Street, and renaming it "Eddie's Lunch." "That," Eddie's son Emile, 75, assured me, "was a real diner." It was a small real diner, however, with a seating capacity of but 18. Five booths were added circa 1929, about the time Eddie closed his Granite Square operation. Then, in 1939, more booths were added, to bring the diner's seating capacity to 65. There was also a pair of dining rooms, total capacity 110, built onto the rear. This, then, was the Eddie's that Arthur Lessard recalls. Darron Pierson, too. Darron, who's 53 and a native of close-by Weare, has fond memories of his family coming into Manchester on a Saturday. "It was a big thing for us kids (Darron and his two brothers) to come into the big city. We'd have lunch (at Eddie's)...a hot dog or a hamburger or fried clams." Darron admits, though, that he was not overly adventuresome. "I would usually have a hamburger. Hamburgers were always my favorite." And, he adds, "Eddie's hamburgers were very good."

Edouard Pouliot died, basically from overwork, at the young age of 53 in November of 1948. His widow, Laura, stepped in and kept Eddie's going until 1952. Then it was their son Gene's turn. He ran operations through 1956, when Urban Renewal came to town and leveled the entire Amory Street area. Eddie's Lunch was not excluded. On the former diner's site there is now the Henry J. Pariseau Senior Citizen Apartment Building.

Photo, circa 1926. Courtesy of Emile Pouliot, Manchester. Eddie's the one with the hat.

Emile also relays that when Eddie purchased the 24-Hour Lunch and transformed it into Eddie's Lunch in 1926, his father served a full meal for 35¢, and that included soup, roast pork, a vegetable, potatoes, coffee and dessert.

Photo, circa 1935. Courtesy of Emile Pouliot, Manchester. Eddie, again, is the one with the hat.

NEW HAMPSHIRE

GOVE'S IMPROVED BARBEQUE LUNCH
HAMPTON FALLS

Bar-b-que was big along the New Hampshire coast in the 1920s, 1930s, and 1940s. Mrs. Gordon Janvrin recollects that when she was a teenager in the 1920s quite a number of bar-b-que stands/joints/eateries "sprang up along Route 1." She's right: there was Bill's, and Paul's ("A Pleasant Place for a Pleasant Taste"), and Gove's just in Hampton Falls alone.

Ira Gove opened his place circa 1928. He'd been a ship-builder in neighboring Newburyport, Massachusetts before he decided bar-b-que was more fun. "The price was 15¢ for a pork, beef, ham, or chicken sandwich and did they taste good," reminices Mrs. Janvrin, adding "Tonic (soda) was 5¢ but Moxie was 10¢ a bottle so I had to think twice before buying a drink."

With wife Minnie doing the waitressing, Ira ran Gove's Improved Barbeque Lunch until he retired in 1940. Minnie then took over and ran the place until she, too, retired, circa 1948. There is, today, no trace of Gove's (or, for that matter, Bill's or Paul's, either) anywhere along Route 1.

"Oh, I remember Gove's. They used to serve these beef bar-b-que sand-wiches on a roll. It was delicious. It was a medium-sized place...not like those big places of today. Actually, I guess you'd call it small." Virginia Small, age 67. October, 1999

Postcard view, circa 1932

It's difficult to be certain, but Harriet Atwood believes the bottom postcard view to be circa 1926 and to be before the relocation; the top view to be circa 1940 and to be after.

124

WAYSIDE TEA ROOM
CHOCURUA

Back in the "Roaring Twenties" Chocurua, as small as it is, was a two tea room town. There was the Riverside and there was the Wayside. Sisters Phyllis (the Riverside) and Alice (the Wayside) Pascoe were the owners and the operators and, of course, the cooks. "It was just plain good old Yankee cooking," ventures 87-year old Harriet Atwood, "because that's what the Pascoe sisters were good at." Their pies were said to have been an especial treat. Harriet confesses, though, that she never ate at either tea room. But the gift shop section at the Wayside: now, that's another matter. She'd often go there - "when I was big enough to walk the mile down and back" - with her cousin Ruth. "We'd go there with our allowance and study the gift case for possible things; beads, necklaces, and the like." That was in the very early 1920s.

In 1928 the state widened Route 16 right through the location of the Wayside. Alice and her husband Quinn solved that quandry by having the tea room jacked up and hauled across the highway. There it existed – as the Wayside; then a grocery store; then a laundry; then a private residence. It was demolished to make way for a new post office in 1999.

From an ad in a 1937 booklet entitled GOOD PLACES TO EAT AND SLEEP IN LEBANON AND VICINITY

WHITE OWL DINER
LEBANON

The White Owl was a fixture at 56-58 Hanover Street in Hough (pronounced "Huff") Square for the better part of five decades. Opened as the Pollard Lunch in the 1920s, it went through several ownership and name changes before becoming the White Owl, with Charles C. White as proprietor, in the early 1930s. The White Owl it remained, surviving a major fire in downtown Lebanon in 1964, before being demolished to make way for a new bridge approach to Route 120 in 1970.

Postcard view,
circa 1958

Photo, circa 1949. Duane's in
the middle with his original
building in the background.

WINDMILL RESTAURANT & CABINS
LACONIA

As with a goodly number of the cafes and restaurants included in LOST DINERS AND ROADSIDE RESTAURANTS, the Windmill's origins were humble indeed. When it opened in 1949, three miles north of Laconia on Route 3, its trio of overnight cabins most likely contained more squarefootage than its restaurant. Seating was limited to 22 at any time, either at highbacked wooden booths or at a counter. The owners were Mae and Duane Thomas and, not surprisingly, they were the operators, too.

Mae and Duane stuck with old favorites such as chicken pot pie, Yankee pot roast, and fried fisherman platters. All

were made from scratch. As the sign over the door promised: "Home Cooking" / "Home Pastries." Mae's pastries were especially noteworthy.

In 1960 the structure pictured here, along with the three cabins, was razed to make way for an ultra-modern and much larger Windmill. It remained in operation, under the guidance of Mae and Duane's son-in-law Jim Carroll, until 1986. The restaurant then changed hands and names – to Dante's – and remained in business three more years until closing in 1989. As of this writing the former restaurant is being used as an antique/junk shop called Gail's Misc.

YANKEE FLYER
NASHUA (cont'd. from page 93)

In 1932 Bill and Chris closed the Main Street Diner, the better to focus on the Yankee Flyer. Business boomed and the duo wrestled with how to best handle it. Their solution: step up to a new and much larger diner. That decision made, the partners went whole hog. They ordered a top-of-the-line "Sterling Streamliner," measuring an impressive 56 feet in length (Yankee Flyer number 1 had measured 36). Seating capacity was 73. Grand Opening Day was January 22, 1940. Again the Diner Duo went whole hog: they sprang for a full-page ad in the *Telegraph* that not only pictured their sleek new eatery, still called Yankee Flyer, but also featured an individual photograph of each and every Flyer cook, waitress, kitchen man, and counterman. A veritable sea of smiling faces. Twenty-four in all! Accompanying wording described the Yankee Flyer as "An outstanding achievement in this form of industrial design." And, with its porcelain enamel exterior, mahogany doors, ceramic tile, "tea rose" Formica, fluorescent lighting, upholstered stainless steel booths, Monel metal sinks, refrigerated salad trays, etc., etc., it most certainly was.

Photo, Yankee Flyer #1, probably 1939. Courtesy of Frank Mooney, Nashua. According to Newburyport, Massachusetts diner historian Donald Laplainte this diner was transported to Newburyport where it sat, up on blocks, through the 1960s. It was then destroyed.

Photo, Yankee Flyer #2, probably 1950. Courtesy of Frank Mooney, Nashua. Just across Main Street from where this beauty once held sway – and the Mural still does – there is today Nashua's sole remaining diner, Joanne's Kitchen. Although disguised on the outside, Joanne's is all diner inside. I especially like the time-worn "Reach for Sunbeam Bread" door push.

With Bill as business manager, his wife Jennie the hostess, and Chris the staff supervisor, the Yankee Flyer thrived through the 1940s. Bill and Jennie retired in 1949; Chris passed away in 1952. Chris' wife Mary Anne then took over and operated the Flyer until 1965, when she sold the property to a group of investors that was planning big things – even a skyscraper – for downtown Nashua. There are those who say that the diner was then moved to either North Chelmsford or Newburyport, both in Massachusetts. But Daniel Zilka, head of the American Diner Museum and an authority on Sterling diners, believes it was not moved anywhere. That it was demolished. I, sad to say, think Daniel is right.

THE MURAL

It's unique – at least to my knowledge – in all the world: a mural paying tribute to a diner. The vision of then Nashua mayor Rob Wagner in 1994, the Mural, which measures an impressive 32' x 8', was funded entirely by private contributions. Featured was a contest to determine who would be commissioned to actually paint the Mural. Nashua native James Aponovich got the nod. And it featured some fancy fundraising on the part of a committee headed by Nashua arts enthusiast Meri Goyette. "We raised $20,000 quite easily," Meri told me, "but we figured we needed $30,000–$35,000." Meri's solution: see if people would be willing to fork up $1,000 to be included in the artwork. They were. One man even paid the $1,000 to have his old car painted into the scene. "That helped put us over the top," laughs Meri.

The Mural, dedicated in August of 1997, is a delight. Authentic, too, with Bill and Jennie Reich, Chris Kyriax, pastry chef/piemaker extraodinaire Alphonse "Fred" Robichaud, others, right there, almost as large as real life. Meri tells me that "The community loves it (the Mural)." But Meri's not completely happy herself. She wants to see a mini-park built around the Mural. "I'd like people to be able to sit and enjoy the art," says she with conviction. I hope she succeeds.

NEW YORK

Area: 49,576 sq. miles.
Population: 18,976,457

Sea Breeze •●

● Akron

● Geneva

● Blasdell

● Silver Creek

Cortland ●

● Dunkirk

● Bath

● Riverside

● Olean

● Waverly

Western New York

Scale: 1 inch = approximately 28.7 miles

Eastern New York
Scale: 1 inch = approximately 43 miles

- Malone
- Rome
- Utica
- Cazenovia
- Amsterdam
- Bridgewater
- Schenectady
- Sharon Springs
- Middleburgh
- Bainbridge
- Leeds
- Johnson City
- Hale Eddy
- Rhinebeck
- Highland
- Wingdale
- Mountainville
- Cornwall
- Carmel
- Garrison
- Brewster
- Ardsley
- Bellmore

Postcard views, both circa 1930. Without the Storm King Highway there'd have been no Bayview Tea Room.

BAYVIEW TEA ROOM
CORNWALL-ON-HUDSON

In the early 1920s Route 218 – better known as the Storm King Highway – was constructed by the State of New York. Running from West Point to Cornwall-on-Hudson, the Highway offered quite spectacular views of the Hudson. Not surprisingly, the Storm King became a tourist mecca. And, equally not surprisingly, there arose a need for places to eat. "Anyone with a house of any size," states Cornwall-on-Hudson historian Colette Fulton, "opened little tea rooms to accommodate travelers." The Bayview, situated at the end of the Highway (*not* 9W, as it states on the postcard), was one of those little tea rooms.

About 1935 the Bayview reverted back to being just a plain old house. And one that fell into disrepair at that. "It had been empty quite a few years. It was a dump." That's how Jeannette Stowe, 84, who purchased the structure with her husband Jerry in 1946, phrases it. "He (Jerry) transformed it from a shell into a home." A very beautiful home, I might add. Over five decades later, Mrs. Stowe still resides in that home, located at 211 Bayview Avenue; still enjoys her view of Cornwall Bay; still lauds the splendor of the Storm King Highway.

BILL'S SERVICE & LUNCH
HALE EDDY

In 1943 the Standard Oil Company of New Jersey hired noted photo editor Roy Stryker to oversee a project that would capture – and improve upon – the image and fabric of Standard Oil. Stryker took his assignment liberally. The end result was a rather marvelous collection of 70,000 black and white photos, shot between 1943 and 1950. This is one of those 70,000. I like it because of its "on the road" feel. Was the photographer – whose name was Charlotte Brooks – coming around the bend in a Chevy? A DeSoto? A Nash? Did she snap this photo and then run? Or did she stop for gas, too? How about a bite or two at Bill's Lunch?

Today's Hale Eddy holds few clues for answering any of the above. Cut through by highways, it is a community of perhaps a hundred souls, situated flush on the New York/Pennsylvania border. Oldtimers recall when there were four stores, several selling gas and eats. Now there are none.

Next stop, Hancock.

Photo, August 1945. Courtesy of Photographic Archives, University of Louisville, Louisville, Kentucky. Bill's stood on "old" Route 17, since supplanted by "new" Route 17 (the "Quickway"), which, in turn, is scheduled to be replaced by Interstate 86.

BREUNIG'S
LEEDS

You could call Breunig's a hodge-podge. Or you could call it multi-faceted. It sold ice cream, candy, and souvenirs. It housed a tea room for many years, and also served sandwiches, coffee, etc. on and off. Then there was its mineral water, too.

Joseph Breunig opened his place just after World War I. He'd run a successful ice cream and candy store in New York City but was advised, for health reasons, to move out of the City. Leeds, 95 or so miles up the Hudson, seemed a good bet. What became his new home had been a second-hand furniture store. Joseph turned it into a palace of sweets. He was especially proud of his store's old-fashioned soda fountain and his wall treatment. The fountain featured a thick white marble counter while the walls were decorated with artificial roses and rose vines.

Also special was Breunig's mineral spring water, sold for 5¢ a glass or 25¢ a gallon. Even better known were the store's ice cream sodas and sundaes, both made with home-made syrups and fresh fruit in season.

Joseph, with considerable help from family, ran his business until after the end of World War II. He then sold to a couple, Elsie and Rudy Ohlsen, who changed names to the Mohican Trading Post. Several owners later the venerable structure is still operating under that name and still selling ice cream and sundaes.

Postcard view, 1934. What was Breunig's is yet in operation today. Joseph Breunig's old marble counter is gone, though. And the wall of artificial roses is, too.

CORNER MAIN STREET AND GREEN LAKE AVENUE, LEEDS, N. Y.   275

BREWSTER CABIN
Intersection Routes 6 and 22
Brewster, N. Y.

7591

Postcard view, circa 1940. When Dick Love opened his Brewster Cabin in 1932 he ran ads that read "If you pay us a visit, we will try to please you." It would appear he succeeded.

BREWSTER CABIN
BREWSTER

Between the regulars at Bob's Diner and the regulars at Brewster Hardware, both fixtures in downtown Brewster, I was treated to Brewster Cabin memories galore. Chet Angioletti, 81, recalls the Cabin as "a roadside place." Bob Heinchon, 74, remembers the steaks. "It was a good steak place," he says. For Frank Tierney, also 74, it was "a nice mix of tourists and locals." Jim Shepard, the youngster at 71, remembers an adjoining log cabin gas station. He thinks they sold Tydol. All of the gang talked of the bands that played weekends. And that there was a sizable heat register right in the middle of the dance floor. "You danced around it most of the time," laughed Bob H., "but if you weren't paying attention or were dancing a polka you could run into it."

The Brewster Cabin opened in the fall of 1932. The Proprietor was Richard L. Love. Ads promised "A comfortable place to eat Home Cooked Food" and "Rest Rooms with hot and cold water at your Service."

In 1946 the Brewster Cabin (aka Love's Brewster Cabin) became the Hollywood Cafe. Ten pairs of nylons were given away as prizes the day of the Grand Opening, June 27th. The venerable eatery operated as the Hollywood until 1965, when another name change was made, to Sciortino's. Sciortino's (aka Sciortino's Hollywood) it has remained. With numerous additions through time, however, any resemblance between it and the view you see here is purely coincidental.

Photo, 1951. Courtesy of Dick Hubsch, Carmel. There's probably a tale behind most every photo ever taken. Here is the tale behind this one. "It was the fall of '51 and I decided to take our new car (a 1951 moss green Pontiac Straight Eight) out for a 'test ride' and eventually found myself on the road to Carmel, to check on our summer bungalow," relates Dick Hubsch, who now lives in Carmel but who then resided in Mount Vernon. "It was lunchtime by the time I got there, so my first stop was the Carmel Diner. I had this old pre-war Agfa box camera with me and it had some film left in it. When I left the diner I looked back (through the rear window) and I saw I could see 'Carmel Diner' and I thought this would make a perfect shot." Voila, fifty years later, here's Dick's shot.

CARMEL DINER
CARMEL

The first Carmel diner – the one on display here – was set up in downtown Carmel circa 1930 by an entrepreneur named Dudley Adams. "He did everything," says Dudley's son Eddie, 75. "He had a taxi business, the school bus business, a painting business, The diner was just one more thing."

Dudley and others ran the diner until 1948 when it was purchased by Max Pearlman and his brother-in-law, Jack Spicak. Max, born in 1913, had grown up working in diners in the Philadelphia area. When he heard from his sister Bea, who owned the close-by Mahopac Diner, that the Carmel Diner could be bought, he jumped at the opportunity. "It's what he always wanted to do: own his own diner," Max's daughter Lenore "Lyn" Woller, 62, told me.

Max bought out Jack in 1950. He was still, though, not content. His diner was "a wooden model...and not in great shape," says Lyn. What Max wanted was his own brand new diner. It was a wish that came true in 1953. Max bought a Silk City (made in Paterson, N.J. by the Paterson Vehicle Co.). "He was proud," Lyn says simply. The old diner, she is almost certain, was demolished.

Max Pearlman ran his "dream diner" in its downtown location until 1967, when he had it moved north of town on Route 52. He moved because he had to. "A couple of big gas companies decided that (Max') corner was a prime site for a station," explains Lyn. Suddenly Max' lease (for the land on which his diner stood) was not renewed.

Max oversaw his diner, always called the Carmel Diner, until it was demolished to make way for a shopping center in 1977. Continuing to cook in this place or that, Max Pearlman lived until 1998. "He just loved to cook," smiles Lyn. Max' downtown site, at the corner of Gleneida Avenue and Fair Street, is now occupied by a gas station/convenience store.

Photo, courtesy of Eddie Adams, Carmel. A smiling Max, circa 1949. He was known for Hungarian goulash, meatloaf, "good diner food," states Lyn. Newspaper ads of the day promise "Finest Food Anywhere" and "Coffee At Its Best." It was a good combination.

Lyn, who waitressed at the diner when she was a youngster, still laughs when she recalls a group of a half-dozen older male customers who would come in for coffee every morning...and argue with each other over who would grow the biggest tomato. "It was so funny," she yet recalls these 50 or so years later.

What does Dick, 77, recall about the diner? That he used to court his wife-to-be, Catherine, over a pair of meat loaf platters, complete with mashed potatoes and string beans or carrots. That he'd always have apple pie à la mode for dessert. That the diner did not suffer from a shortage of windows. "What was nice," Dick reminisces, "was that it (the diner) had so many windows. No matter where you sat you had a good view."

Ad, CORNING / PAINTED POST CITY DIRECTORY, 1941. Private showers, New, Clean, Comfortable. And guests who wrote glowing words. That was Crystal City.

CRYSTAL CITY RIVERSIDE

If competition and/or lack of business doesn't get you, maybe a hurricane and/or flood will. Such was the fate of Crystal City.

Opened in late 1938, Crystal City took its name from nearby Corning and its fame as a cut glass center. It was located in the Village of Riverside, about ¼ mile over the Painted Post line heading for Corning on old Route 17 (now Route 415). Reuben T. Pierce, formerly co-owner of a building and plumbing supply house, was proprietor. Overnight cabins – "Airy In Summer/Heated in Winter" – were the primary attraction, but ads also promised "Home Cooked Meals." A separate building – the Diner and Bar-B-Q Building – was opened in 1940. It was not to be a success story. Within two years Reuben T. Pierce folded the eatery part of his operation.

Memories of Crystal City do not abound. To most older local residents it was just a place that was "there." As Robert C. Wiley, 81, of Painted Post put it: "There were cabins. Tourists would stop." Anthony Speciale, a 77-year old Corning resident, was the only person I could find who actually ate at Crystal City. He recalls that the food was "good." And Nick Tostanoski, 76, and also a Corning native, remembers the Crystal City as "a nice place," continuing: "It was built good; they kept it good; and they were doing (in the 1940s/1950s) good business." But Nick never ate at the Crystal City.

Hurricane Agnes – and the devastating flood that came with it – caused the end of scores of Corning / Painted Post/Riverside businesses when it swept through in June 1972. Crystal City (then owned by a Mrs. Ella de Lorraine) was one of them. By later in the same year there was a McDonald's on the site. That, too, was eventually done away with, to make way for the Southern Tier Expressway. Where the cabins – "Airy In Summer/Heated In Winter" – and the diner/bar-b-q used to stand, just west of Buffalo Street, there is now a grassy field.

Postcard view, circa 1940. When it opened in 1940 the Crystal City Diner and Bar-B-Q was one of 63 eateries in operation in the Corning/Painted Post/Riverside area. The count would soon revert back to 62.

CRYSTAL CITY CABINS Between CORNING & PAINTED POST

DINER & BAR - B - Q

CRYSTAL CITY CABINS

DAIRY ISLAND DAIRY BAR
BLASDELL

The Dairy Island Dairy Bar was born in 1946 as a sister operation to Arcade Farms, a Blasdell dairy farm with roots that stretched back to the turn of the century. The Dairy Island offered a new and direct way for Arcade to market its milk and, especially, its ice cream. A local favorite was a "black and white sundae" (vanilla ice cream smothered in chocolate syrup). Other favorites included the usual hamburgers, grilled cheese sandwiches, BLTs, and French fries. Lifelong resident Jim Baker, 65, recalls that the Dairy Bar was a favorite gathering spot after school and after church on Sundays. But, he adds, "It was right on the main thoroughfare to and from the City of Buffalo and so it (the Dairy Bar) got a lot of commuter business as well."

In the mid-1950s the Dairy Bar was closed and its space converted to dairy production. It was eventually, in 1988, demolished. On the site there is today a parking lot.

Postcard view, circa 1950. "It was right on the main thoroughfare to and from the City of Buffalo."

Dairy Island — 3807 SOUTH PARK AVE. — BLASDELL, N. Y.
— TWO MILES FROM BUFFALO CITY LINE —

DANNY'S DRIVE-IN SCHENECTADY

"They had carhops and they'd put a little tray on your window. They had A&W Root Beer. That was a longtime ago." So sums up 78-year old Jerome Prener, the only person I could find with any recall of Danny's at all. And it *was* a longtime ago: when World War II had come and gone and all of America was seemingly in their auto and on the move. Schenectady was there. So was Jack Goldstein. Jack had Danny's built in 1948 on the outskirts of the Electric City. On New York Route 5, a straight shot to and from Albany.

Danny's sold root beer, chicken in the basket, hamburgers and hot dogs, frosteds and malteds until 1956. Since then what was begun as Danny's has assumed many names: 4 Mac's. the New Holland Inn, Martha's, Anthony's Restaurant. On the site there is now an eatery called the Golden Dragon. How much of its structure dates back to the days of Danny's Drive-In? How much does not? Only Jack Goldstein would know for sure.

Matchbook cover, circa 1950. Jerome Prener remembers the root beer. But he doesn't remember the roller skates.

GATESDALE DAIRY BAR
BRIDGEWATER

The Gatesdale is a survivor. It was founded in 1941 by Carlton "Tubby" Gates and his wife Beatrice. "Tubby" was a member of the Gates' family, owners of a long-established dairy farm in central New York. Naturally enough, the milk for the dairy bar's ice cream came directly from the Gates' farm.

Carlton and Beatrice ran the dairy bar until their retirement in the late 1960s. Several succeeding proprietors tried their hand. Results were mixed. Then, in 1997, area natives Sharon and Dick Brooks bought the Gatesdale and set about restoring it to its past grandeur. The couple installed color fluorescent lighting that shines out the building's large plate glass windows and brightens the dining room, too. They gave both the interior and the exterior a sound refurbishing. And they covered (but didn't do away with, Sharon is careful to note) the words "Dairy Bar" with the word "Diner" in their resplendent outside sign. That's to reflect the fact that the Gatesdale is now far more than a dairy bar. While you may still order the Soup Bowl Sundae (five large scoops of ice cream topped with chocolate syrup, marshmallow, and nuts), you may also fill up with homemade soups, a wide range of omelettes, daily specials, and/or, if it's Friday night, the Friday Night Fresh Haddock Fish Fry.

Sharon and Dick, both in their mid-fifties, are also proud of their sign. (It's the one that's difficult to miss in the postcard view on the facing page!). While the *building* you see in the view was built – to replace the original – in 1951, the huge *sign* is straight out of 1941. It's a beauty, too, complete with lights that blink to give the impression that milk really is flowing out of that bottle and into that glass. If you are ever on the Cherry Valley Turnpike (U.S. Route 20) in the vicinity of Bridgewater / West Winfield, be sure to admire the sign. And then stop in. Have the Soup Bowl Sundae. If it's Friday, have the Haddock Fish Fry. Better yet, have both.

Gatesdale Dairy Bar   **U. S. 20**   **Bridgewater, N. Y.**

Postcard view, circa 1962. Sharon recounts the story of a couple who recently stopped by: they were retracing their honeymoon route of fifty years earlier and were "ecstatic" to find that a place where they'd enjoyed ice cream all those years ago was still open. And still in business.

GUY C. LIGON'S WINGDALE DINER - ROUTE NO. 22, WINGDALE, N. Y.

BEER on TAP

70 miles to NEW YORK
30 " " POUGHKEEPSIE
25 " " DANBURY

Postcard view, circa 1940. "They (the diner) had lots of locals. Tourists, too, would stop. Once you went in there they knew you were going to come back. It (the food) was that good." John More, July 2000

GUY C. LIGON'S WINGDALE DINER
WINGDALE (DOVER)

Town of Dover (Wingdale is a part of the Town of Dover) historian Donna Hearn *thinks* the Wingdale Diner opened sometime after the Harlem Valley State Psychiatric Hospital was built in the early 1920s. She *knows* it was originally owned by Guy Ligon; later by Linton Weil. Other people I spoke with agreed. But what those other people really wanted to talk about was the food. "Damn good food," states 71-year old Dover native John More. "It was the way they prepared it," he elaborates. "Their steak was my favorite. It was about 1" thick. It was perfect." As for Guy Ligon: "He couldn't do enough for you. He always wanted to know how everything was."

Stanley R. O'Dell, 73 and also a lifelong Dover resident, doesn't disagree. His favorite was the roast beef, with mashed potatoes, peas and carrots. "It was like good home cooking." Then there's 62-year old Doris Johnson: her husband George "swore by the (diner's) meatloaf."

The diner – later converted to part diner/part bar – was operated through the 1970s. It then sat vacant until 1986, when a couple named Jack and Marilyn Hughes bought it and turned it into a combination package store and beer/soda outlet. Today the building, located just a mile south of the present-day Adam's Diner on Route 22, looks not unlike it looks here.

HARBOR DINER
DUNKIRK

Gertrude G. Giebner oversaw her Harbor Diner for 30 years plus. As Gertrude's grandson, Ron Giebner, 47, tells the story: "Gertrude and her husband (John) owned a farm in Sheridan (just east of Dunkirk). One day she told her husband she was sick of living on the farm. She packed up her kids – all six of them – and moved to Dunkirk. There she ran a boarding house. Everybody enjoyed her cooking. They called her 'Ma' Giebner. They gave her the idea of opening an eatery."

Ron's a little sketchy as to when all this happened, but DUNKIRK CITY DIRECTORY listings indicate it was the late 1920s/early 1930s. It *is* known that by 1934 Gertrude and her Harbor Diner were rolling, with "Ma's" cooking pleasing customers far and wide. Pies were special. "She was famous for them," recalls her daughter, Thelma Messere. Another favorite was her chicken dinner. Ron yet recalls the dinner's mashed potatoes and gravy. "Rich gravy," he says with a smack of his lips.

Gertrude G. Giebner ran her diner through 1964. Business was never the same after the Thruway opened in 1959. "She lost a lot of trucker business," states Ron. In 1964 Gertrude sold to Thelma, who converted one side of the Harbor to a bar. She changed the name, too, to the Harbor Inn, and operated it through the 1980s. It was then purchased – and destroyed – by the City of Dunkirk as part of an Urban Renewal project. On the site, 2 Lake Shore Drive, there is now a City Pier boat storage area.

Postcard view, circa 1950. Courtesy of Tom Hug, Vermilion, Ohio. I talked with a lot of Dunkirk "oldsters" who well recalled the Harbor Diner. I especially liked Pat Sweet's recollection: "My husband and I were breakfast regulars in the late 1940s and early 1950s. He'd have ham and eggs up and home fries and I'd have a sandwich they'd build layer by layer for you: bacon, sharp cheddar cheese, fried egg, etc., all served on a homemade biscuit. They had a breakfast sandwich before there were breakfast sandwiches."

Cleanliness — Good Coffee

Harbor Diner — Lake Shore Drive — Phone 2550 — Dunkirk, N. Y.

HOLLYWOOD HOTEL
SHARON SPRINGS

When it comes to fine eats there have been many jewels across New York's 375-mile stretch of U.S. Route 20. One of the most enduring is the Hollywood Hotel. Opened in 1929, just two years after Route 20 had been designated a national road (It spans the continent, running from Boston to Newport, Oregon.), the Hollywood was a place you'd be sure to include when out for a Sunday spin in your Hupmobile or Studebaker. "Customers came from as far as Syracuse, Albany, Schenectady, Gloversville and that area," fondly recalls longtime proprietor James Bowmaker. Bowmaker, now 84, is a native of Sharon Springs. "As a young man I worked there (at the hotel) as a dishwasher for $1.00 a day," he relates. His dream was to one day own the hotel. That "one day" arrived in 1957.

With himself the chef ("There were 14 meats and 12 assortments of seafood on the menu.") and his mother, Elizabeth, the pastry and pie chef ("Her pies were famous, especially her pecan and apple pies."), the Hollywood was mealtime heaven. Sold by Bowmaker in 1972 ("I was just burned out with the restaurant business."), the Hollywood Hotel continues in operation to this day, a wonderful throwback to leisurely drives and Sunday dining.

HOLLYWOOD HOTEL, SHARON SPRINGS, NEW YORK 81

7A-H1257

Postcard view, 1937. Today's Hollywood is known as Perillo's Hollywood.

Ad, CORNING TELEPHONE DIRECTORY, 1936-1937

HOTEL WAGNER
BATH

I know the Hotel Wagner and its Moroccan Restaurant weren't really "roadside," but this is such a wonderful period advertisement I couldn't resist including it. The Hotel Wagner opened its doors on November 2, 1925, the pride and joy of Walter Wagner, a native New Yorker who'd moved from New York City to the Bath area as a child. Hotels were his love, and he owned and operated several of them in Bath and nearby Avoca before unveiling his crowning achievement, the hotel that bore his name.

The Hotel Wagner was originally three stories, with a fourth added in the 1930s. There was a Chrysler showroom on the ground floor for a number of years. A bustling dining room served meals, both to local residents and to tourists and business people passing through town on Route 17 or 64.

The hotel, located at 115 Liberty Street, operated until 1967. It has since been converted to an office building.

HOWELL'S DINER
GENEVA

This is a diner, it's wonderful to be able to say, that is definitely not "lost." It is, after years of heartbreak, going strong as Patti's Lakeview Diner. And if you want diner-proprietor enthusiasm…you talk to Patti!

Before we do talk to Patti, though, let's go back a few years. To 1933. That's when what is now Patti's opened as the Texaco Grille (please see page 103), an adjunct to a next door Texaco gas station. The diner's original proprietor was Don L. Woodworth (please see page 106), who'd come to Geneva from Hornell. Woodworth operated the diner until early 1945 when he sold to a F. Wesley Tuxill (who doubled as a Geneva fireman). Ads during Tuxill's regime ballyhoo the diner's day and night service and the Grille's

Sunday breakfast: "It's pleasant, enjoyable and economical – and saves so much trouble around the house on the day of rest."

The Texaco Grille was purchased by Harry Howell in March 1954, becoming Howell's Diner. Harry's ads often featured a howling (as in "Howelling") dog. Clever. A fire caused the diner's closing in 1968. Fortunately, though, the structure was saved. It has since seen service as Goebert Automobile Supply, NAPA, and, finally, as a diner again. In 1996-1997, Geneva native Patti Guererri completely refurbished the veteran building and, much to Geneva's delight, opened as Patti's Lakeview Diner.

Postcard view, circa 1950. Courtesy of Geneva Historical Society, Geneva. The Texaco/Howell's/Patti's Lakeview is a Bixler diner, built by the long-defunct Bixler Manufacturing Co., formerly of Norwalk, Ohio.

NEW YORK

Photo, July 2000. Located at 43 Lake Street, just off Routes 5 and 20, Patti's Lakeview lives up to its name: it's but a stone's throw from Seneca Lake, the largest of the Finger Lakes. Next door, as an added treat, is the former Texaco station, constructed in 1922, and still resplendent under its roof of red Spanish tile.

Photo, July 2000. "I love the people who come in," beamed – and I mean beamed! – Patti Guererri, 50, when I asked her how it's been, owning and operating the diner. She quickly added that she loves old buildings, too. Especially old diners. Makes sense: her mom worked at the former Murphy's Diner in Geneva when Patti was but a kindergartner. "I helped fill the salt and pepper shakers," she laughs.

In 1980 Patti and her husband Frank bought the former Texaco/Howell's. They left it, however, as an auto supply store. Not a handsome auto supply store at that: the former diner had been covered over in the late 1950s. "It was an attempt to modernize. But it was ugly," states Patti. "I always kind of wanted to open it back up (as a diner.)."

In 1997 Patti's wish came true. She and Frank "unmodernized" the facade and completely refurbished the interior. Patti gladly shows before and after photos. Grand Opening Day was President's Day, 1997. For Patti, it seems, it's been a grand day ever since.

Photo, circa 1959. Courtesy of Jim Baker, Hamburg, New York. That's Lou in the front door.

LOU'S DINER
BLASDELL

"It didn't have air conditioning or the other modern amenities, but if Blasdell residents or the many commuters along South Park Avenue wanted a good wholesome meal at a reasonable price they eventually would find Lou's Diner." So wrote Town of Hamburg (Blasdell, just south of Buffalo, is part of the Town of Hamburg) historian Jim Baker in his "Out Of The Past" column in *The* (Hamburg) *Sun* in September of 1995. Lou's patrons would, continued Jim, "appreciate the casual conversation as well as the 10-cent cup of coffee and the full course dinner for $1.15. That dinner included meat, potato, salad, vegetable, bread, and cof-

fee. Early morning coffee drinkers were sure to be reading the *Buffalo Courier Express*, delivered by 6 a.m. each morning to a green *Courier* box at the diner's front door."

I think Jim likes diners. And it sounds like Lou's was a good one. Lou (short for Lucille) McNally, a lifelong Blasdell resident, took over what had been Dave's Diner in 1953. The structure, with 13 stools, a counter, and a kitchen, is believed to have dated to the 1930s. Lou, with help from her daughter Mary Lou, ran it to 1968. By then the diner was worn down. It was demolished in 1970. In its place there is today a parking lot.

LYKE'S
CAZENOVIA

"Tasty Sandwiches"/"Hot Coffee"/"Good Sunday Dinners" /"No Gambling Devices"/"No Punch Boards." So read a Lyke's ad from October 1937, just after Harry Lyke opened for business. Similar ads followed most every week in the *Cazenovia Republican*. "Home-Baked Pies and Rolls. Delicious Sundaes. Plate Luncheons = 35¢. Full Course Thanksgiving Dinner = 85¢." Lyke's covered most all the bases. And the consensus among Cazenovia's "oldsters" is that Lyke's was successful. "The restaurant was always full. You had to go early to get a table" is what they say. Yet, come 1941 or so, people seem to remember that Harry packed up his family and moved to Rochester. Nobody remembers why. His location, at 82 Albany Street/U.S. Route 20, is today occupied by an antique shop.

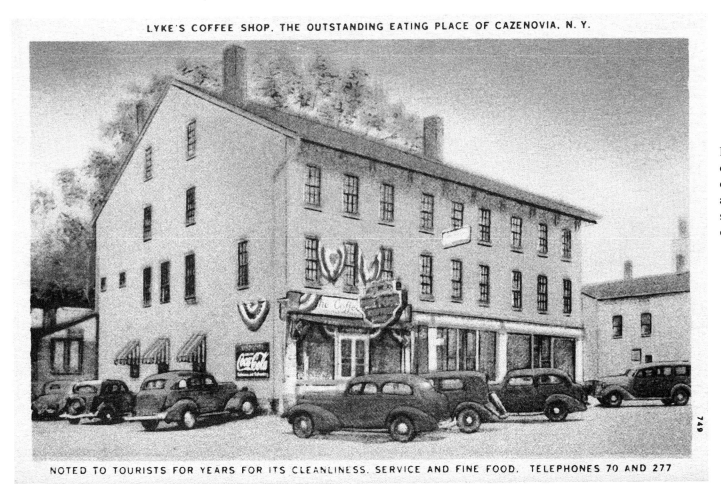

LYKE'S COFFEE SHOP. THE OUTSTANDING EATING PLACE OF CAZENOVIA, N.Y.

NOTED TO TOURISTS FOR YEARS FOR ITS CLEANLINESS, SERVICE AND FINE FOOD. TELEPHONES 70 AND 277

Postcard view, circa 1940. Fans of Coca-Cola will appreciate the sign on the side of the building.

MIDDLEBURGH DINER
MIDDLEBURGH

Ervin and Anita Shelmandine owned and operated Shelmandine's Restaurant, on Main Street in Middleburgh, from 1924 to 1945. They then retired. Erv, though, was not the retiring kind and, in 1950, he and partner Bill Feeck built the Middleburgh Diner on Route 145, again in Middleburgh. At first it was small, seating perhaps 35. Still, the meals were good and the word spread. Almost before you knew it, people were taking a Sunday drive from as far off as Albany and Schenectady to eat at the Middleburgh Diner.

In the fall of 1951 Erv and Anita's daughter Barbara and her husband Stephen bought out Bill Feeck. Now the diner was a family affair. Their pies, proclaimed to be "Like Mother Used To Make," were a specialty. Helene Farrell, 78, well recalls those pies. Especially the cream pies. And the apple pie. And the crust. "Their crust was really great. It was flaky. It was light. It was good."

Since 1989, when the Shelmandine family decided it was time to really retire, the diner saw several operators come and go before Luis Patino and family came to stay in November 1991. "They rejuvenated it," says Helene, "and it is a busy community diner."

Postcard view, most likely 1950. The diner is still called the Middleburgh, (Sometimes also spelled Middleburg – as here – on and off through the years.). There have been some additions here and there, but by and large the building still looks pretty much as it does here.

Middleburg Diner

ROUTE 9-D, GARRISON-ON-HUDSON, N. Y.

Postcard view, circa 1954. Located on Route 9D, 2.8 miles south of the Garrison post office in a section called Manitou, what was Mom's looks today much as it did here...except the gas pump is gone, the signs are gone, and the business is gone.

MOM'S RESTAURANT
GARRISON

Town assessor records show that Daniel and Margaret ("Mom") Romanello purchased the structure that became Mom's in 1945. It had been a house. Before that, again per town records, it was a "roadstand." Soon it was a restaurant. "It was the only place (to eat) between Peekskill and Cold Spring," relays Charles Bartnik, who's 64 and who lives just across the road. "They did a good enough business to make a decent livelihood." Ice cream, sandwiches, steaks, chops, breakfast: it was all on the menu. Plus those famous pies. "We used to have hamburgers and apple pie. She (Mom) was big on apple," Charles remembers back.

"Or maybe I was big on apple," he adds. The Romanello's – often just called "Mom" and "Pop" – also sold a fair amount of Sinclair gasoline. So recalls the Romanello's nephew, Bill Walsh, 43. Bill even recalls Sinclair's "Drive with care and buy Sinclair" slogan. We both got a good chuckle out of that.

The Romanellos sold Mom's in 1972. Since then the old "roadstand" has been, alternately, vacant or used as a delicatessen. It is now vacant.

Photo, circa 1922. Ed's on the left; Bill's on the right. Their Valley View Farms' stand is behind them.

O'BRIEN'S WAVERLY

From a hot dog and soda pop stand to one of the better known roadside restaurants in the northeast…that's the tale of O'Briens. It all began in 1918 when brothers Ed and Bill O'Brien opened the small Valley View stand pictured here on their parent's property outside of Waverly. And if the stand was small, so were the brothers. Ed was all of twelve; Bill weighed in at eleven.

By 1926 the brothers had outgrown the Valley View. They purchased the former Hill's Cafe in downtown Waverly and transformed it into what they at first called O'Brien's Lunch; then the Log Cabin. In 1937 Ed and Bill aimed their sights a little higher. Literally as well as figuratively: they abandoned downtown in favor of a brand new cafe they had built high atop Waverly Hill, 1,100 feet above the Chemung Valley.

The last step in Ed and Bill's restaurant journey came about by chance. Ed, in the Marines during World War II, was stationed in San Diego. There he noticed the many restaurants with large picture windows. "If San Diego can do it, so can Waverly," he wrote Bill. In 1946 Ed's vision became reality. The brothers built their fourth and last building on the crest of Waverly Hill. It featured huge Thermopane windows and twenty-mile views. Considered by some to possess "America's Most Scenic Dining Room" and recommended by Duncan Hines (Remember him before he became the name of a cake mix?), O'Brien's was, by all accounts, a splendid place to dine.

In 1964 Ed and Bill added a motel. In 1965 Bill retired (he would die in 1969). In 1988 Ed retired (he would die in 1996), leaving O'Brien's to his son, Ed, Jr. Ed, Jr., however, elected to go his own way, putting most of his time and energy into his position with Corning, Inc. (formerly Corning Glass). The result was predictable: O'Brien's closed in 1997. As of this writing the grand old eatery, located on Route 17C (the old Route 17), has been re-opened under the ownership / management of the Paul Mitchell family. The name, however, remains the same: O'Briens. "Why would I change it?" asks Paul, who's 50 and who grew up in nearby Sayre, Pennsylvania. "It's a landmark."

BEER AND ALE

Schaeffers	45c
Budweiser	45c
Schlitz	45c
La Batts Ale	45c
Ballentine Ale	55c
Blatz	45c

This is the beer list from an O'Brien's menu of April 1953. While the prices are right, the spelling is not. How many mistakes can you find? Answers below.

("Schaeffers" should be Schaefer's. "La Batts" should be Labatt's. "Ballentine" should be Ballantine.)

O'BRIEN'S RESTAURANT
ON WAVERLY HILL, WAVERLY, NEW YORK

Postcard view, 1947. On a clear day you can see two states, fourteen counties, and twenty miles. Ed and Bill called it their "Twenty-Mile Mural."

155

PETER MAZZA RESTAURANT
AKRON

The artwork portrayed here could make a person thirsty. And Peter Mazza's did quench thirsts. But it satisfied appetites as well.

Italian-native Peter Mazza purchased what had been the Oak Cafe in 1915 as he was approaching his 20th birthday. The Oak Cafe name remained in use for awhile, "but," laughs his daughter Pam (Mazza) Casseri, "eventually everyone just called it 'Pete's.'" Pam remembers that chili, hot dogs and, especially, roast beef sandwiches ("He was noted for his roast beef.") were the house specialties. She also recalls, proudly, that during World War II her dad would treat all Akronite servicemen home on furlough to a roast beef sandwich, chili, and a beer.

By 1947 Pete Mazza was wearing out. He sold the business he'd run for 32 years. And died two years later. The building that was his home as well as his business – he and his family lived upstairs – is today still in use as a restaurant/ tap room called the Filling Station.

Matchbook cover, circa 1945. In addition to "Good Foods" and "Cooler Keg" Beer could be added "Peanuts." Pam recalls that every Friday morning Pete would drive to Buffalo and come back with two big ("really big") bags of unshelled peanuts. "It was his way of treating his customers. It was like hors d'oeuvres. And they (his customers) loved it."

PICKUP'S DINER
OLEAN

"Pickup's" may seem an odd name for a diner. Unless your name is "Pickup" and you happen to own the diner. Such was the case with Estes Pickup. Born and raised in Springville and Little Valley (both in western New York), Estes moved to Olean in 1917. For three years he worked as a jeweler. Then he ran a grocery store. Somehow, though, it was diners that were really in Estes Pickup's blood and, in 1929, after operating dining cars in Batavia and East Aurora, he purchased an existing diner in Brooklyn (definitely not in western New York) and had it transported to Olean.

Estes' diner was a success and in 1932 he moved it to a larger site in Olean. In 1937 Estes moved his diner one last time, to 242 North Union Street, in the midst of downtown. He also constructed an annex, working hard to duplicate his original structure. He then "framed" the two together, as shown here.

People in Olean well recall Estes Pickup and his diner. Estes is remembered as "a big person"/"always congenial"/"happy go lucky." Sloppy Joe's

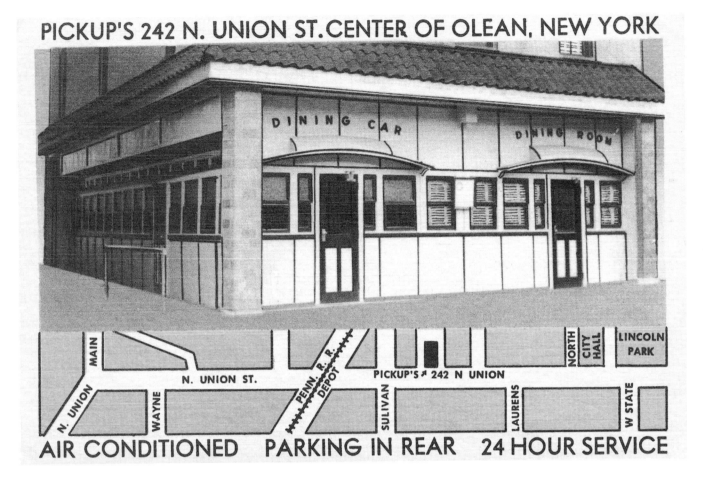

PICKUP'S 242 N. UNION ST.CENTER OF OLEAN, NEW YORK

DINING CAR

DINING ROOM

N. UNION MAIN

WAYNE

N. UNION ST.

PENN. R. R. DEPOT

PICKUP'S 242 N UNION

SULLIVAN

LAURENS

W STATE

NORTH

CITY HALL

LINCOLN PARK

AIR CONDITIONED   PARKING IN REAR   24 HOUR SERVICE

Postcard view, circa 1950. The name "Olean" comes from the Latin "Oleum," meaning "oil." The Olean area – plus adjacent northern Pennsylvania – was America's pioneer oil-producing region.

are the menu specialty most vividly recalled. As relayed by lifelong area resident Ann Martin: "They had the first (Sloppy Joe's) in the area that I can remember…and they were *huge*." Ann also recalls that, when she and her co-workers stopped in for coffee, "This one waitress, Mary, would get our coffee when we walked in the door: she knew just the way we liked it."

In 1969 the Pickup family sold their "double diner" to a local couple named Emil and Ceile Haynoski. Business was

not what it had been, however, and in 1971 the diner, still called Pickup's, went bankrupt. It was then purchased by Jack Blumenthal, owner of a variety store next door. Jack added on to the former diner, re-did its facade, gutted the interior, and created Blumenthal's, Inc., a camera and computer complex. So Pickup's still exists. Sort of. Even that may come to pass, however, as it appears highly likely the complex will be bulldozed to allow for expansion of the Olean branch of Jamestown Community College.

157

Photograph, June 21, 1938. Courtesy of the Weber Collection, The Queens Borough Public Library, Jamaica.

REST INN
BELLMORE

Picture field and forest and you're not likely to picture Bellmore, located on Long Island's south shore. When what became the Rest Inn was built in the late 1860s, however, it was built as B.F. Sammis' Sportsman's Hotel, a lodging house and eating hall for the many hunters and fishermen that came out to what was then the country for a respite from New York City. The structure later became the Garden Rest, and, then, in August of 1937, the Rest Inn, the name it enjoyed when this marvelous photograph was taken 60+ years ago. More recent names have been the Triangle Restaurant, and the Smithville Cafe. The long-standing eatery still operates today as the Smithville Cafe, located at the intersection of Bellmore Avenue and Bellmore Road.

STAR DINER
MALONE

Malone's Main Street is also U.S. Route 11, *the* major artery serving New York's North Country. The result: the Star Diner, located at 114 East Main, saw considerable passing-through-town business. "We had a lot of truck drivers and salesmen," well remembers former proprietor Carl Steenberge. "Lots of salesmen from all over the country. We were famous for our apple pie."

The Star opened its doors, circa 1942, at a location that had previously housed Taro's Restaurant and then Tim's Restaurant. Tim's proprietor was Gene Timmons, who was also mayor of Malone at the time. Several proprietors later Carl, who's now 76, came on the scene. That was 1947.

"We served regular restaurant fare," he says. Hot roast beef sandwiches, grilled cheese, hamburgers and French fries and, of course, coffee. "We sold a lot of coffee and doughnuts," Carl smiles. "We always had four great big urns (of coffee) going." Homemade pastries and muffins went over well, too. Plus that apple pie. To top it off, Carl made his own ice cream.

The Star's name was later changed to the 49er Restaurant. Carl bailed out in 1952. "Our landlord kept raising the rent," he explains. The block that housed the diner was destroyed by fire in the late 1950s. On the site today is a Key Bank.

Main Street looking West, Malone, N. Y.—8

7B-H1983

Postcard view of Main Street, Malone as it appeared in 1947. The Star Diner is on the right. The Star may be gone, but a rather nifty Malone eating institution lives on. It's Sansone's, located at 321 East Main Street, and it's been a local favorite since 1939. What I especially like are the old checks that have been framed and hang here and there around the restaurant. I noticed one from 1948 that totaled to a $4.00 charge for 16 beers. Try finding that kind of check today!

SWEET CLOVER FARMS MILK BAR
MOUNTAINVILLE

The Seaman family, originally from Long Island, had owned and lived on a large tract of land in Mountainville for well over 100 years before Charles Seaman founded a dairy farm on it in 1917. He gave his endeavor the inviting name of "Sweet Clover Farms." Seaman's most notable customer was the U.S. Military Academy, located just south in West Point.

In 1930 Charles and his son Jim went a step further and established home delivery service, retailing milk and the like to a sizable area around Mountainville and Cornwall. Eight years later, in July 1938, the Seamans gave their sales an even bigger boost when they opened what was described in *The Cornwall Local* as "a resplendent milk bar." Milk, milk products, sandwiches, and fruit were the milk bar's staples, with a customer base that included both area folks and, as *The Local* put it, "the tourist trade." In 1948 the entire operation was purchased by Cornwall resident Vincent Borthwick. It was not a good move. Small dairies, as with small breweries and small soda bottling works, got badly hammered by the big guys in the 1950s. By 1960 Sweet Clover Farms was no more.

Postcard view, circa 1946

WESTCHESTER DINER
ARDSLEY

I lived seven of my most formative years in Ardsley and graduated from Ardsley High in 1958. The Westchester Diner was long-since gone and forgotten by then, replaced in town by a wonderful establishment named the Chocolateria (always called "the Choc."). Hamburgers were 15¢ and so was the egg cream of your choice (chocolate was mine). So for 30¢ you had a "complete" lunch.

Let us return, however, to the days of the diner. It was owned and operated by Angelo DeMilo. That's his wife, Anne, and son, Charles, looking sharp for the camera. Charles (called "Pete") is the one on the tricycle. Now 71, he recalls the diner vividly. That it was small and narrow; that everything – the grill, steam tables, large coffee urns, etc. – was right in front of the patrons; that his father made a great pea soup; that pie (apple was the most popular) and coffee was 15¢.

The Westchester Diner was opened by Angelo DeMilo in 1927. Angelo, who was born in Italy in 1896 and came to America in 1910, had served in the U.S. Army during the Great War. After the war he worked at various jobs, but cooking was the one he liked. "It's something he thought he could do," relays Pete. And, in fact, Angelo did it so well that by 1929 he was the owner of five restaurants in

lower Westchester County. Then came the Crash and Angelo was forced to sell off four of the five. You can guess the one he kept: the Westchester. There he did ok. But it was a struggle. In 1933 Angelo's landlord had Angelo move the diner so that it sat perpendicular – rather than parallel – to Ardsley's main street, Saw Mill River Road/U.S. Route 9A. That hurt, notes Pete, because "you couldn't see the diner (while) driving through."

Angelo DeMilo continued to serve pie and pea soup and a whole lot more at his diner until 1940. Then he heard about what seemed to be a better restaurant opportunity "upcounty" in Yorktown Heights. He went for it, moving to Yorktown Heights and operating his new place, the Wagon Wheel Rest, until he retired in 1960. He died in 1987.

As for the old Westchester Diner, Pete remembers that his father had it jacked up, loaded onto a flatbed truck, and taken away. He doesn't know where it was taken. It was "kinda sad," says Pete.

Photo, circa 1934. Courtesy of Fred Arone, Dobbs Ferry. Anne and Pete – with Pete looking less than fully enthralled – and the diner. (Ed. note: the NRA placard in the window stood for the National Recovery Administration, not the National Rifle Association.).

THE WHITE HOUSE
ROME

Rome's been home to its fair share of diners. The grand-daddy of them all, though, was almost certainly the White House. Francis X. Donovan, Curator of Photographs at the Rome Historical Society, believes the White House may go back to as far as 1899. The name of its first proprietor(s) has been lost through time. It is known, however, that a man named Leo F. Bauer purchased the White House in August of 1920, and that his son, Elmer F. Bauer, joined in the business not long thereafter. As is evident in the photo, the White House came equipped with a full set of wheels. It appears from city directory listings of the day, however, that Leo and Elmer parked their lunch wagon at 106 West Liberty Street and left it parked there. The walkway, the steps, and the grass around the wheels would support that.

What began as the White House later, in 1936, became the Liberty Lunch and then, in 1941, Funzi's Diner (after proprietor Funzi Aricco). It closed on November 1, 1969. Remarkably, no substantial alterations were made to the structure in all its many years of operation. It was demolished circa 1972.

Photograph, circa 1920. Courtesy of the Rome Historical Society, Rome.

"White House" was a lunch wagon model first produced in 1890 by the New England Night Lunch Wagon Company (later the T.H. Buckley Lunch Wagon Manufacturing and Catering Company), located in Worcester, Massachusetts. They were generally, notes Richard J.S. Gutman in his book AMERICAN DINERS THEN AND NOW, sixteen feet long, six to seven feet wide, and ten feet high. That's not real big. (Try pacing off your kitchen to see which would be larger: your kitchen or the White House.).

Photo, 1941. Courtesy of the Library of Congress, Washington, D.C. At its peak in the mid-1950s White Tower operated 230 units, serving their famed "Buy a Bagful" hamburgers from Boston to Minneapolis. Their Amsterdam outlet, open from 1935 to 1956, was one of the 230.

WHITE TOWER AMSTERDAM

I am not a fan of chains. I don't like their sameness. I don't like their absentee ownership. Somehow, though, I've never let that dislike prevent me from favoring White Castle and White Tower. Plus there are several ingredients that make this photo an especial favorite. For one thing, there's the wonderfully nonchalant look of the waitress. Then there's the last bite – was it the hamburger for 5¢? – nearing the mouth of the woman-with-hat. The abundance of signage is a plus, too.

The photographer who took this Library of Congress shot in October 1941 noted that the White Tower was "the liveliest place in town." He/she was probably right.

Pawtucket •

Providence

East Providence •

Saunderstown •

RHODE ISLAND

Area: 1,214 sq. miles.

Population: 1,048,319

Scale: 1 inch = approximately 6.1 miles

17150

BABBIE'S CABINS
Plum Beach, Rhode Island

Postcard view, circa 1940. Hot dogs were 5¢. Hamburgers were 15¢.

BABBIE'S
PLUM BEACH (SAUNDERSTOWN)

Edwin and Edith Babcock celebrated Memorial Day 1921 by opening a one-room hot dog and hamburger stand on Boston Neck Road (later to become U.S. Route 1/now U.S. Route 1A). They called it Babbie's. Hot dogs were 5¢. So was soda. Hamburgers went for 15¢, relates Edwin and Edith's daughter, Helen (Babcock) Dwelly. The stand was open on Sundays only. "That was the day people went to the beach or for a drive," further relates Helen. Clam chowder and clam cakes, both prepared by Edith, were other house specialties.

Babbie's was a summer-only operation until 1934. That's when Edwin lost his "real" job, as local postmaster, and the couple decided to winterize their building, move in, and remain open seven days a week and all year long. They also added the sale of groceries and gas, and constructed overnight cabins, too.

"Babbie" and "Mrs. B," as they were often called, ran Babbie's for over 50 years. Circa 1973 they sold to Helen and her husband Bill. Helen and Bill kept longer hours and added additional gas pumps. But, notes Helen, it was the "same old building."

Eventually, modernity called and the "same old building" (the one pictured here) was demolished, in the 1970s, to make way for a new model. It still, as Heffie's, operates today.

LOVELY'S DINER
PAWTUCKET

"Checkered" is how to best describe the life and times of Lovely's Diner. Lovely's #1 opened in 1929 at the corner of East Avenue and Church Street when George F. Lovely took over operation of a lunch wagon that had been run by one Albert Cassidy since 1925. "But it was hit by the Crash," George's grandson Joe Lovely, Jr. told me. The result: this initial Lovely's shut down before 1930 had run its course. As to what happened to the wagon, Joe, Jr. thinks "It was put on wheels and rolled away someplace."

A second Lovely's, located at nearby 50 Pleasant Street, fared no better. Opened in early 1931, it closed by late 1931. "It was a lovely (no pun intended, I'm sure) diner," per Joe, Jr., but it, too, suffered from the Depression. "Everything went to hell," as George's brother and former counterman, Jim Lovely, 87, puts it more emphatically. The fact that the city was in the process of digging up the roadway in front of the diner didn't help, either.

It would not be until 1947 that another Lovely's Diner was opened. George F. Lovely, who'd overseen attempts one and two, had died in 1934. But his son, Joe, and his grandson, Joe, Jr., kept the dream alive. Back at the original location, too. It so happened that a second diner – after Cassidy's/Lovely's lunch wagon was moved – had been set up at East Avenue and Church Street and operated under various names – Balser's Diner, Delmonico Diner, Frank's Diner, Brothers Diner – from 1932 on.

During World War II the diner, as with many another, suffered from meat, butter, etc. shortages. A butcher from Attleboro, Massachusetts, again per Joe, Jr., bought the diner, but made the mistake of trying to run it from Attleboro. It didn't work. "He was robbed blind," says Joe, Jr. In stepped Joe, Jr. and Sr., in 1947, with $5,000.00 in hand. Voila: Lovely's #3.

Ad, *Pawtucket Times*, May 23, 1930, for Lovely's first diner at East Avenue and Church Street.

Lovely's #3 was a success for an impressive 27 years. Joe, Sr. died in 1955, but Joe, Jr. kept rolling. "We were a cut above other diners," he states proudly. "We charged a little more…but it was worth it." Joe fondly recalls that all the cooking was done right out in front. "It was like show business." Even a break in the action – Urban Renewal reared its head in 1966-1967, necessitating a move from East Avenue – didn't slow Joe down. He transported the diner to a new site at 200 South Bend Street, in the shadow of McCoy Stadium (home of the AAA Pawtucket Red Sox), and kept on rolling. Until 1974, anyway. "It was 1974," relates Joe. "There were long gas lines and very high interest rates and we weren't making any money. It was too much work for nothing." Joe, Jr. sold the diner. Today, Joe, Jr. has retired to Syracuse. And his former diner? It's, with additions to it, still at 200 South Bend, still in the shadow of McCoy Stadium, and still (as the Right Spot Restaurant) in operation as an eatery.

Lovely's as it appeared circa 1960. Courtesy of
Spaulding House Research Library, Pawtucket.

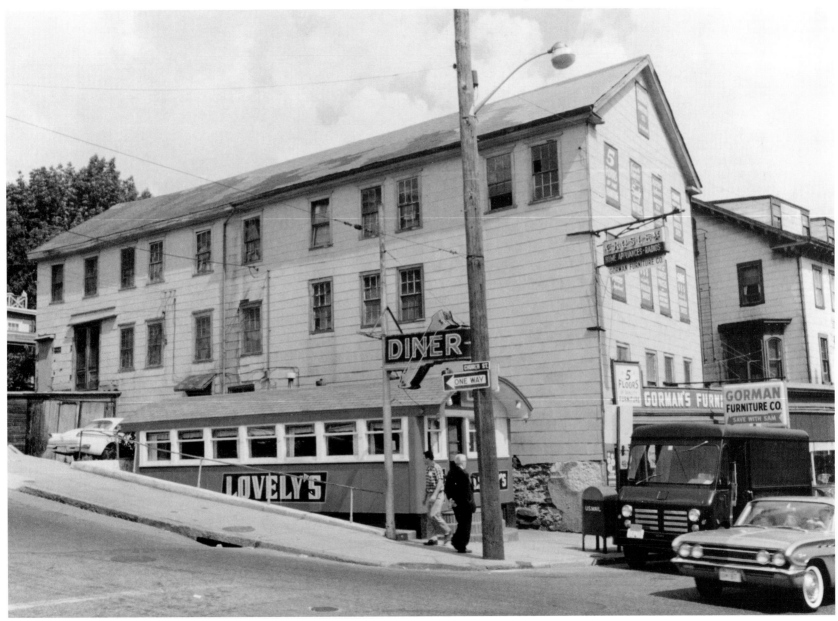

Postcard view, circa 1935. Courtesy of Tom Hug, Vermilion, Ohio. Russ' favorite "believer" is 63-year old Seekonk, Mass. native Joan Champigny, a long time Crescent Park devotee. Joan points out that many of the Park's attractions changed names from year to year. She and others she's rounded up recall the structure shown here as being in Crescent Park...but they recall it by names other than the Rose Garden. "Call it what you may...but call it within Crescent Park" is what they say.

THE ROSE GARDEN
EAST PROVIDENCE

What's a guy from East Stroudsburg, Pa. doing hanging around Rhode Island? The answer: trying to solve the Mystery of the Rose Garden. The "guy" is Russ Irwin, a friend and fellow roadside enthusiast. When I mentioned that I had a marvelous postcard view (see left) that had no place to call home, Russ took it upon himself to do some serious investigating.

There was little doubt that the view was New England, what with Ipswich clams (the Ipswich area of Massachusetts has long been noted for its clams), shore dinners (basically a New England tradition), and broiled live lobsters (something you're not likely to find in, say, Wyoming). And the "Radio Station WPRO" wording (see over the triple set of windows beneath "Shore Dinners") certainly sounds for all the world like Rhode Island (as in "PRO" for PROvidence). Given all these clues, finding the Rose Garden's location looked to be a piece of Johnny Cake. However, a thorough search through each and every RHODE ISLAND BUSINESS DIRECTORY from 1910 to 1950, correspondence with WPRO (founded in 1924; still in operation in East Providence) and reference librarians from throughout the Ocean State all came up empty.

Enter Russ, who spent the better part of ten months "on the case," and his findings: findings formed after four trips to New England and extensive communication with most anyone who was willing to talk with him. Then there was the telephone and E-mail. And more telephone and E-mail. Russ' conclusion is that the elusive Rose Garden was within or right outside Crescent Park, an amusement park of considerable renown (It was billed as "The Coney Island of New England."), in operation in the Riverside section of East Providence from 1890 to 1979. It is not a definitive conclusion. Russ is the first to admit that. But it is a conclusion that he – and I – feel comfortable with. There's 92-year old Louise Gormley of Narragansett. Louise took one

Russ about to enter his "adopted" state, April 2000. "I seem to be learning more than I care to about a lot of places I've never heard of," he told me, adding "but I'm having fun as well as frustration."

look at the Xerox copy that never strayed far from Russ' side and she, without hesitation, placed the Rose Garden in Riverside. Numerous older former Crescent Park employees would point and say "That's where the Rose Garden was." Others, however, would point to somewhat different sites. Part of this confusion is undoubtedly due to the everchanging aspect of the park. Rides and attractions were moved/torn down/replaced from one season to the next, both within the 56 acres that comprised the park and on the perimeter, too. Then there's the matter of time. Seventy or so years is a lot of decades ago.

So we'll go with Russ' best bet: that the Rose Garden was in or immediately outside Crescent Park, Riverside, East Providence, Rhode Island.

TIMES SQUARE DINER
PAWTUCKET

I caught up with 75-year old Pawtucket native Frank Santos as he was killing time before going to the YMCA. I'm glad I did. "This brings back memories," he grinned when I showed him a copy of the photo pictured here. "I remember their boiled dinner," he said right out. "It was very good. Not overcooked. Not mushy. And it was plentiful. That's why they did the business they did."

Frank's memories, which are from 1945-1947, would have been music to Antonio Donati's ears. It was Antonio who founded the Times Square in 1934. Far better known as "Tony," Donati's life reads like an Horatio Alger epic. Born in Catanzaro, Italy in 1893, Tony came to America and Rumford, Maine at age six. At age 12, in 1905, he traveled to Pawtucket to visit an acquaintance; couldn't locate the acquaintance; was befriended by a policeman; was taken to the Boston Fancy Bakery on Main Street; was introduced to the bakery's owner, Charles Giusti; was offered a job at the bakery by Giusti; accepted the job. It was the start of a lifelong love affair with food handling and preparation.

After service in the U.S. Army in World War I, Tony Donati went into business as proprietor of the Puritan Lunch on Broad Street. In his adopted Pawtucket, of course. Then, in 1934, Tony made the big move: to the Times Square.

Later Times Square owner/operator Tom Soukas describes the Times Square as having been an "old-type diner...kind of a mongrel, put together to fit that particular spot." Per Tom, 66, who owned it from 1970 until its demise in 1975 (Tony Donati died in 1958. He was followed as diner pro-

There was a man from Pawtucket,
Who kept all his cash in a bucket;
But his daughter named Nan,
Ran away with a man,
And as for the bucket, Nantucket.
—R. A. L., '34

Limerick from the February 1932 issue of *The Killonian*, the magazine of Killingly High School, Danielson, Conn.

prietor by his widow Alice; then Edwin Feeley; then Tom), the Times Square was also primitive, with no heat, no air conditioning. "When a truck drove by the diner's lights would flicker," laughs Tom. The kitchen was in the basement, with a low ceiling. "Good thing I'm not tall," laughs Tom again.

Still, though, Tom (who presently owns/operates Tom's Restaurant at nearby 29 Summer Street) clearly has a great affection for his former eatery. He talks of how he fixed it up; hired the first female counterperson; sold copious quantities of corned beef, fresh ham, fish and chips, and eggs. Especially eggs. "We had a lot of fun," he sums up. "I miss it."

Photo, June 1957. Courtesy of Spaulding House Research Library, Pawtucket. The Times Square took its name from its proximity to *The Pawtucket Times*. As in New York City, the area around *The Times'* building took the name "Times Square." The diner certainly qualified: *The Times* was right next door. It's the tall building to the left in this photo. And it's still there, serving Pawtucket and surrounding communities. In fact, you can still see the diner's roofline – but not the diner: where it stood is an empty lot created when the structure was condemned and demolished by the City of Pawtucket in 1975 – marked on the side wall of *The Times'* building. It is more than just a little eerie.

VERMONT

Area: 9,609 sq. miles.

Population: 608,827

Scale: 1 inch = approximately 21.9 miles

Morrisville •

Shelburne •

St. Johnsbury •

• Barre

• Manchester Center

• Bennington

Brattleboro •

KNOTTY PINE RESTAURANT
BENNINGTON

The Knotty Pine was a part of the roadside parade that burst across America in the years following World War II. It was opened circa 1947 by former Rutland Railroad clerk Bill Shanahan, Jr. and his wife Jeanette. At first, per later proprietor Donat Ratelle, "It was just a roadside hamburger stand." Then, in 1955 or 1956, the couple added a dining room. A handful of years later, in 1960, Donat purchased the restaurant. Again per Donat: "I guess they (the Shanahans) were just tired. They were getting pretty old." Donat, a native of Woonsocket, Rhode Island who came to Vermont ("There wasn't much happening in Woonsocket.") in 1946, expanded the kitchen but otherwise left the

Knotty Pine as it was. Traditional "family food" was served: chicken, steaks, chops, spare ribs, and the like. Donat, now 82, was proudest of the crowds on Easter Sunday and Mother's Day. "We were full from the moment we were open until we closed," he states.

Donat sold the Knotty Pine in 1967. It was later demolished to make way for a chain restaurant called Carroll's Hamburgers. After that flopped this newer structure was converted to an American Legion post, which is what it still is today.

Postcard view, circa 1958. Note the screen for the Bennington Drive-In Theatre in the background.

NEW MOON DINER

LOUIS DEMAS and OCTAVE C. LOSO, Proprietors

Barre's Leading Eating Place

229 NORTH MAIN STREET   BARRE, VT.

WHEN IN BARRE, STOP AT THE

NEW MOON DINER

HOME COOKING, CLEANLINESS, QUALITY AND SERVICE

The Large Diner on the Square

Phone 816

"We – the employees – could eat whatever we wanted. Except for the scallops or T-bone steak. That's because they were 75¢ for a complete meal. Everything else was 40 or 45¢."

Larry Lawson, short order cook, 1947-1949

108,000 Cups of Coffee sold in 6 Months—Why?

From a 1929 New Moon ad.

NEW MOON DINER
BARRE

I spoke with three men who'd done some cooking at the New Moon. Each, not surprisingly, has his own special memories. Larry Lawson, 68, worked at the diner in the late 1940s. He was proud of the food ("It was all tasty.") and the friends he made. And he has a "coffee story" that made us both smile: "We used to open up at 4:30/5:00 (AM) and the first thing you'd do is make coffee. The second thing – weather permitting – was to open all the windows and doors wide to get that coffee smell out into the street. You'd pick up customers that way. Especially in the summer with tourists coming through."

Francis Rogers, 75, worked at the New Moon in 1951. He recalls that the diner still had wheels underneath it from its old mobile days. As for the New Moon's food, he characterized it as "just an old-fashion little bit of everything."

Kenneth Brault, 65, worked in the diner in the mid-fifties. He recalls it as "a pretty lively place," especially on week-end nights when people would come pouring in after the bars and dance halls closed, and the New Moon was open until 3:00.

The New Moon came into being in 1927, an outgrowth of a lunch cart that had been owned and operated by partners George Gignac and Francis Devine since 1924. Under a host of different proprietors it served Barre for close to 40 years, until the mid-sixties saw its end. By then, as put so well by Larry Lawson, the diner had lost its street trade. Whereas people used to be out and about downtown, "as time went by people got cars and places opened up out of town and people," explains Larry, "went out of town. There just weren't that many customers anymore."

The New Moon was demolished in 1986. Its former site, "On The Square" at 229 North Main, is today yet another parking lot.

Postcard view, circa 1962. Old fashioned chicken pie was the Sunday favorite.

PAINE'S RESTAURANT
MORRISVILLE

"Paine's takes pains to please" was their slogan. And it appears that George and Irene Paine succeeded. The couple opened their place in July of 1950. At first it was called Paine's Dairy Bar and consisted of a six-stool counter and a six-booth dining room with a pair of large tables tossed in. All three meals were served as well as hefty amounts of ice cream: sundaes, ice cream sodas, milkshakes, and banana splits. Irene remembers the banana splits took a long time to make but that "it was a good (selling) item."

Circa 1953 George and Irene enlarged their seating capacity and changed their name to Paine's Restaurant in order to reflect a more full-meal menu. Fried clams became a big seller. So did chicken pie (all chicken/no vegetables). It was served Sunday only and Irene recalls it was so popular that they often ran out by 3:00 PM. The most popular Sunday of them all? Mother's Day. That was the one day of the year that George and Irene took reservations, and they'd still have people standing in line for a shot at a table. What Irene, now 86, also well recalls is the restaurant's most noted customer. That was Alfred Hitchcock, in Morrisville to shoot scenes for THE TROUBLE WITH HARRY in 1954. "He'd come for noon dinner. He always had steak and a salad and coffee. The waitress tried to suggest dessert but usually he declined."

In 1965 the Paines sold out. "We were both worn out," confesses Irene. The former restaurant, located on Routes 12 and 100, sat vacant for a while, then became a gift shop. It is now utilized by radio station WLVB.

TRAVELER'S REST
MANCHESTER CENTER

A full course chicken dinner for 75¢. Five gallons of gas for an even dollar. Was it heaven or was it Manchester Center? It was Manchester Center, of course. At the Traveler's Rest. In the late 1920s.

The Traveler's Rest opened in the spring of 1926. Its proprietor, E. (Ernest) J. Vallee, saw to it that it opened with fanfare. Ads in *The Manchester Journal* rang out "It's A Wonderful Place To Eat," and continued: "When you're working hard all morning you are hungry, not for regular restaurant cooking, but for good home cooking, with plenty of variety. We serve home cooked food in large helpings. Let us do the hurrying, while you enjoy your food."

Before long E.J. Vallee (also spelled, in one place or another, "Valley" and "Vallie") had transformed his restaurant into a night spot as well. Spring/summer 1928 ads touted Vallee's Dance-O-Land as the place to "Dine And Dance And Be Merry."

Patrons of the Traveler's Rest enjoyed the end of Prohibition in the spring of 1933. E.J. served Horton's Real Pilsner (a shortlived New York City brand) on draught. There was dancing every evening (a photo from mid-1933 shows a good-sized dance floor surrounded by linen-table-clothed tables) and "The Best Food In Town."

For reasons unknown, E.J. Vallee closed his Traveler's Rest in 1934. He later operated a grocery store/meat market in Manchester Center. His former restaurant and dance spot became a hardware store, before being eventually torn down to make way for what is now known locally as "the Crystal Palace," a large structure housing a collection of outlet stores.

Photo, probably 1926. Courtesy of the Manchester Historical Society, Manchester. The Traveler's Rest, located at the intersection of Cottage Street and Routes 11 and 30, purveyed Socony gas as well as meals and a dance floor. Socony, later merged with Mobil, stood for Standard Oil Company of New York.

Part of an ad, 1937, showing Willoughby Diner number two. Picture this as a bookstore and you'll picture what it is today.

Photo. Courtesy of the Fairbanks Museum, St. Johnsbury. The original Willoughby as it appeared when opened in 1928. That's probably E. Lloyd McKee on the right; his son (and chef), Ernest H. McKee, on the left. Note also the wonderful octagonal structure in the background. It's still there, serving as an office building.

VERMONT

WILLOUGHBY DINER
ST. JOHNSBURY

Some days sure don't go the way you planned them. Take that day in 1960, for instance, when Sherm Warren paid a visit to his local bank. "I went up there to see about a loan on a candy (vending) route," chuckles Sherm, now 74, "and the bank talked me into taking over the diner. They had foreclosed (on the diner) and they wanted to get rid of it. So I ended up in the diner business."

Sherm's diner had roots that stretched back to 1928, when veteran St. Johnsbury lunch car owner E. (Ernest) Lloyd McKee had a brand new diner brought to town. He had it set up at 48½ Eastern Avenue, in the heart of St. Jay's downtown. There it thrived as the Willoughby Diner, named in honor of nearby Lake Willoughby. Ads touted the diner as "The Popular Eating Place," and the "Most Modern Diner In Northern Vermont," and promised the big three of "Quality Food/Rapid Service/Popular Prices."

E. Lloyd McKee closed his original Willoughby Diner in 1936, replacing it with a spiffy right-up-to-date Sterling diner (manufactured by the J.B. Judkins Co., Merrimac, Mass). This new diner, still called Willoughby, had a new address, too: 28 Eastern Avenue. There McKee's success continued. But it took a toll. He ceased being open around the clock in 1940. And sometime between then and 1947 he sold his diner. For several years it was operated as Lindholm's Diner, a branch of a "parent" Lindholm's in Rutland. It was then, with periods when it was vacant, the Splendid Diner / Splendid Restaurant, until Sherm took over in 1960.

Sherm's first order of business was to transport the diner to a spot in front of his house at 69 Portland Street/U.S. Route 2. "I had a big front lawn," he laughs. The proprietor of a next-door motel, however, saw little to laugh about. He filed suit, claiming noise from the diner would disturb his customers. A court case ensued, with Sherm the winner. Sherm's second change was to re-name the diner the Talk Of Town. "Everybody was talking about the diner – because of the court case – so I figured we'd name it that," explains Sherm.

As the Talk Of Town the diner enjoyed a second heyday. Sherm was an excellent cook and, by all accounts, a great host. "Congenial;" "Nice guy;" "Never an empty coffee cup": these are words people use to describe Sherm Warren. By the late 1960s, however, Sherm's enthusiasm was on the wane. "My wife hated it...the diner's long hours," he says.

In 1970 Sherm sold the diner. The structure then saw service as a real estate office; later an apartment. In 1994 it was purchased by a man named Rick Fayen. Rick gutted the diner's interior, exposing the woodwork behind the walls and ceiling. Months of renovations were followed by the installation of shelving. In late 1995 Rick opened as the Reader's Choice Bookstore, specializing in quality second-hand volumes. "I threw open the doors and wondered where all the people were," he bemuses.

Five years later Rick is still in no danger of being overrun by paying customers. But he gets enough business to make a go of it. Plus he enjoys the social/intellectual aspects of the store. Do people still come in and say "I remember when this was a diner and I ate here?" "They sure do," states Rick. "And I've never once heard anyone say they had a bad meal. It (the diner) was an important and enjoyable part of their memory."

Postcard view, circa 1948. Would A. Chapin Wright, one of whose specialities was "flash cooked doughnuts" (doughnuts that were partially cooked, set aside, then finished cooking just before serving), be impressed with the fact that his restaurant has been torn down and replaced with a Dunkin' Donuts? I doubt it.

WRIGHT'S GRILL
BRATTLEBORO

Finding anyone with any significant recall of old-time Brattleboro can be difficult. Everyone, it seems, is a transplant. Then I found Ken Carpenter, 57, the proprietor of downtown Brattleboro's Town Rexall Pharmacy. "I grew up next door (to Wright's)," he beamed. "I was a little kid then. I used to go in the back door and they'd let me help myself to their homecooked French fries. They were good!"

Ken beamed, too, as he remembered A. Chapin Wright, the man behind Wright's. "He was a tall, lanky, baldheaded fellow. (He'd) chew the fat with you and give you a good portion of home cookin' kind of food."

A. Chapin (the "A." stood for Andrew. Few ever used it, though: he was "Chape," short for Chapin, his mother's maiden name) Wright was "a man of many ventures," as his daughter Cynthia puts it. Born in 1894, Chape had owned and operated a garage, an auto dealership, a tire store, and an insurance agency before setting up Wright's Grill in 1938.

Wright's was a success for a solid dozen years. Early 1940s' ads read "Famous For Clams And Scallops," but Wright's was actually best noted for its steaks. And for a concoction named "Elephant's Delight:" a scoop each of vanilla, chocolate, and strawberry ice cream, topped with hot fudge, butterscotch syrup, strawberry syrup, real whipped cream, and, of course, a cherry. All for 39¢! Cynthia waited on tables as a young teenager in the late 1940s and she recalls "I would do five or six Elephant's Delights an evening." Cynthia also recalls that she hadn't grown much by that time, and that she'd get "lots of tips because people felt sorry for the short little girl."

A. Chapin Wright sold his restaurant, because of family health problems and the need for money, in 1951. He later retired to Florida where he passed away in 1989 at the old age of 95. His restaurant did not fare as well. It was operated, as the Maple Leaf Restaurant, by Keene, New Hampshire resident Peter Evangelo, until 1959. In the mid-1960s, recollects Ken Carpenter again, the structure was jacked up and both moved to its left and turned around. It then served as home to an auto rental agency and, separately, a bar named Mort's Roadhouse, before being demolished in the mid-1970s. On the site there is now a Dunkin' Donuts.

Photo Sources

The majority of the postcard views, photos, ads, matchbook covers, etc. in LOST DINERS AND ROADSIDE RESTAURANTS is from my own collection of "stuff," supplemented by items loaned by collecting friends Peter D. Bachelder and Tom Hug, and the Maine Historic Preservation Commission. Plus other materials, from both libraries and museums, and personal collections. There is a credit line beside each graphic that is not from my collection.

Information Sources

I tried to blend, as much as possible, oral history (i.e., interviews with restaurant proprietors and their relatives, employees, customers, interested bystanders) and "hard" facts. Primary sources for the latter included, where available, the city directories of the day and the local newspapers of the day. I received considerable help from many libraries and historical societies; no help at all from others. The director of one Massachusetts' historical society let it be known that her society didn't consider anything to be of historical significance unless it was 100 years old. So much for Lindbergh's jaunt in the Spirit of St. Louis, Bobby Thomson's "Shot Heard 'Round The World," and World Wars I and II.

For diner information and inspiration I relied upon Richard J.S. Gutman's AMERICAN DINER THEN AND NOW (*the* bible of diner history), plus Michael Karl Witzel's THE AMERICAN DINER, and HOMETOWN DINERS by Robert O. Williams.

For drive-in information it's difficult to top CAR HOPS AND CURB SERVICE by Jim Heimann and THE AMERICAN DRIVE-IN by Michael Karl Witzel. Ditto Chester Lieb's MAIN STREET TO MIRACLE MILE for all-around info. Also very helpful were the several publications of the Society for Commercial Archeology (especially Larry Cultrera's Diner Hotline column), and most everything put out by the American Diner Museum (coming into being in Providence, Rhode Island under the direction of Daniel Zilka).

INDEX

Going, Going...?

Clockwise from upper left: abandoned diner, Boothbay, Maine; abandoned roadside restaurant, Barcelona, N.Y.; diner converted to living space, Springfield, Maine; abandoned diner, Pittsfield, Mass. All photos summer/fall 2000.